SPIRITUAL AWAKENING

How to Grow, Change Your
Worldview, and Build the Life You
Want Without Worry or Judgment.

Jacob Olimash

TABLE OF CONTENTS

INTRODUCTION

A spiritual awakening is a renewal of greater knowledge and awareness of the mind. The spiritual awakening process brings about a personal change and a change in the worldview. When someone undergoes a spiritual awakening, they experience a change in their mindset.

What Causes A Spiritual Awakening?

A life-changing occurrence produces for many a spiritual awakening. It is a slow and subtle change for some.

A traumatic experience

This one affects our physical or emotional well-being profoundly, negatively. A long period of recovery is also followed. Examples of a traumatic experience may be a form of violence or a serious accident.

Major life-changing events

Some experiences will make a difference in your whole life. An incident that changes life could include divorce or the death of a loved one, or a severe illness.

An existential crisis

Often referred to as the soul's Dark Night. The meaning and intent of life start to be challenged during an existential crisis. It often is accompanied by depression or an event that changes life, although this is not always the case.

Experience of almost death

It's quite self-explaining. Many people who mentioned getting an NDE even talk to beings from the other side about coming into touch. Such an experience changes one's perspective on life in-depth, you can imagine.

A Natural Awakening

It's an unintentional awakening method. It occurs after a practice that causes a change in conscious consciousness.

- Meditation
- Care
- Developing a deep link to the care of plants and animals Practices that can stimulate a more conscious sensibility
- Practice of self-transformation.

The process of spiritual awakening is crucial to remember that it is different. Here, however, is an idea of what you might feel.

The Initiation

You will begin to face inner turmoil or a feeling detached from this world at the beginning of the spiritual awakening. You can also grow an ego-consciousness apart from you and recognize greater energy at work in this universe.

This initiation into the awakening journey also follows an event or encounter that changes lives. You'll be asked to look inside during this period and begin the self-evaluation process.

The Query

Spiritual awakening opens your eyes to healing-needed areas of your lives. You will transition through a questioning cycle when confronted with restricting convictions and negative behavioral habits once the process is underway. If you have followed a religious path, you could also encounter this belief system dismantling as you attempt to understand this universe.

The Quest

You will begin to inquire about different spiritual practices on the road towards spiritual awakeness as a way to become aware of the divine knowledge and to dedicate your understanding of this universe. This can be done by going to spiritual prayer centers, reading holy scriptures, or looking for other religions.

The structures of religious faith give us many pathways towards spiritual wakes. Many religions give us a great starting point before we stand on our own feet. The Noble Eightfold Path in Buddhism, for example, describes steps for complete peace (Nirvana).

This world has far more wisdom and complexity than any other religion would contain. This can lead you to a search for several religious practices, or you can also follow a hybrid approach by following values from several different religions.

Integration

On your spiritual path of awakening, light sheds upon your soul's wounds to seek healing. As these wounds become apparent, you are compelled by conventional therapies, divine advice, coaching, and spiritual healing methods to seek assistance.

As you seek healing and direction, you clear negative thinking patterns and make divine insight and wisdom. Healing helps to change the mind into a new mindset.

Oneness With The Universe

You can feel a feeling of unity with the universe at this stage. You can lose your sense of yourself (or separateness from the universe). This is represented in psychology as the ego's death. Ego death is a total loss of self-conception or self-identity.

CHAPTER 1: SPIRITUALITY AND ENLIGHTENMENT

One of the reasons why spiritual awakening is so misunderstood is that we struggle to define the correct words.

Ken Wilber offers nine valid meanings of spirit and spirituality in A Sociable God, for example.

We sometimes relate "spirituality" to religious contexts, but this is problematic in my expertise. Let us now describe the spiritual as a quality that goes beyond the physical and material spiritual realm.

Light may also mean many things, but cognition is most commonly linked to it. Via disciplined analysis of higher spiritual values, you can have an "illuminated mind." But this illumination does not suggest that you are spiritually awake or mentally aware.

Therefore, Spiritual awakening is an awakening of a level of truth beyond the ego. The ego is our only sense of being or "I."

This awakening happens when the ego somehow makes a Higher Self or Spirit come up inside for some purpose.

The average person is more than the human person. The ego is mostly a set of archetypes, programs, or behavioral patterns. The Taoists call this set of programs the mind that we have acquired—a global state since we were born.

Spiritual awakening involves the re-emergence of what the Taoists call the Original Spirit or the so-called Self. And it is this Spirit return that makes us genuinely human.

Spiritual Awakening vs. Mental Awakening

The terms spiritual awakening and mental awakening are often commonly mistaken.

Psychological awakening concerns pineal stimulation. With it, you open up to other realms beyond this restricted three-dimensional world of time and space.

In comparison, Spiritual awakening entails opening the core of the heart. It's a psychological, emotional, and soul mechanism more closely linked.

What are the Spirit and the ego?

The ego thinks it's responsible, or what the Taoists call the lower spirit.

It's our self-centered sense or "I."

- "I'm [your name]" when you say something like that.
- •"I've got [job, home, car, wife, child]'
- "I [insert a thinking], I guess."

That is the ego. This is the ego. It's possessive because it feels separated from everything else.

The lower soul is guided by simple pleasures, negative feelings, and the basic human needs of Maslow. The lower soul's hunger is insatiable and goes on for eons if it is left unchecked.

He referred to his ego when Maslow said, "Man is a perpetually desperate beast."

Fortunately, the Spirit, the Higher Self, or the Higher Soul is there as well. And these fundamental needs are not the driving force of this divine flame. It is instead calm, neutral, merciful, intelligent, and intuitive.

The Spirit is still in a state of being, while the ego is always.

Here's what happens when we awaken spiritually

We appear primarily to associate with the ego.

The ego is then submerged to the soul as the process of spiritual awakening takes place... The lower soul becomes the higher soul, in the terminology of Taoism.

Jung's process of individualization aimed to achieve this Spirit or psychic wholeness.

But this usually does not occur in a single 'moment of awakening,' despite the common opinion. While "speak experiences" can open us up to a Self-transcendent truth, these are brief experiences.

Instead, the literature on development describes that there are psycho-spiritual stages of growth. And over time, these constant phases begin to evolve.

And that's so many people are disturbed by the spiritual awakening. For example, they may have a lovely experience of unity, walking in nature, or on a psychedelic drug, but this experience is momentary. The composition of the individual's consciousness has not yet changed.

Spiritual traps: Spiritual awakening False Signs

Therefore let's study the typical false signals before we go through the genuine symptoms of spiritual awakening.

1: You are "good" thinking, and some are "bad."

This belief is deeply ingrained in most of us as it is a typically Western religion curriculum taught.

Shadow work is necessary to uproot this assumption. When you stop comparing everyone, you will know you have undone this restricting conviction instead of seeing yourself in anyone you encounter.

2: Identification of you as a "Spiritual Being."

In religious and new-age circles, this false identity is universal. You are not both spiritual and material. You overcome them, and they are all included.

It is a sign of spiritual ego or inflation to identify as a spiritual being. 3. Searching for "Love and Light" will allow you to see again that you're no better or different from any other.

"Love and light" or "goodness" is another deeply embedded program in the teachings of the religious and new age that prevents genuine spiritual growth. The "spiritual" action produces a person or a social mask, making others feel like we are "good people." While the individual will raise our status and increase self-confidence, he does not promote spiritual or psychological development.

In reality, spiritual awakening comes from the opposite direction where, since childhood, we face in ourselves the terror, rage, guilt, and grief. Taking these encounters into account paves the way for authentic spiritual growth.

4: Nice's Acting

A pleasant act is an indicator of psychological immaturity and not a spiritual awakening sign. It's told to "be good" and behave ourselves, by our parents and different institutions (school, religion...). And we meet this request to different degrees, thus strengthening the shadow hand.

If you behave good, this is a certain indication that someone is manipulating you. (Usually, the original manipulator or trickster is a parent, but it's in you now.) A mature adult does, though, without needing other people's approval.

5: You believe secretly that you are better than others

Maybe you can see a trend here: all these traps indicate ego inflation. Spiritual awakening motivates us in our humanity, but spirituality is often another instrument to disassociate, judge, and grandiose...

Often this trap happens when:

- Read a lot of spiritual texts
- Join a spiritual or religious group
- Start a spiritual practice
- Find a spiritual teacher

Another ego game is unique.

Be highly alert when you think you've "found it." This is a symptom of a particularly early stage, not an indication of spiritual awakening, psychological growth.

All these signals of the subconscious point to vampire feel.

Beware of the Spiritual Bypass

The "spiritual bypass" is perhaps the biggest trap in the spirituality game.

Spiritual principles and practical methods are used here to prevent mental or psychological injuries unresolved. These injuries need to be tackled to continue our psycho-spiritual growth.

We also oppose this phase because it involves the pain they serve to face these wounds.

These injuries are primarily traumas in childhood. Almost every emotional cause you had was definitely from your past in your current setting.

"The dreadful has already occurred," says Heidegger.

A large number of persons fall into the spiritual bypass pit in different East and West religions. For much of my thirties, I did too.

Spiritual Signs of Recovery

Now that we have examined some of the wrong signs of spiritual awakening let us revisit some of the real signs.

1: A Noticeable Change in Your Behavior

Maybe in your everyday behavior, you will notice the most important and real signs of spiritual awakening.

The ego or lower soul's signs are compulsive, neurotic, and addictive conduct. No such tendencies occur in the spirit or the higher self.

The Spirit is not motivated to satisfy the fundamental needs as it's already total and complete. So when you experience completeness or okay, it's a positive sign of spiritual awakening moment by moment.

And due to this all right, without attempting to do so, you will genuinely be more infantile (and less responsive) to others.

See also: Any behavior change: Impulse Control

2: Emotional wellbeing is deepening

Perhaps the key thing that blocks spiritual awakening is disturbing our emotional body. The Jungians call it an impairment. When we resolve childhood emotional trauma, we reverse this injury that lets us feel deeper and more truly.

The re-engagement of this emotional flux affects all aspects of our life. Now we are more authentically human instead of being possessed by a host of archetypes.

There is less resistance to feeling like that (even negative emotions we resisted before). There is an increasing willingness to face emotions such as terror, anger, and remorse rather than sedation.

3: A Slow Down and Return Tendency

To develop the above signs, self-reflection is important when you reverse the present. In modern times this reflection is difficult because of the fast pace we seem to be running. There is a push for success, efficiency, and optimum results, but they soon become symptoms of neurosis... The facility may be our companion for spiritual awakening.

So you will start to slow down and think more often as a spiritual awakening symptom. A desire comes to life in you to understand yourself and your conduct more clearly. The Buddhists call it a halt and a halt.

Retraction allows us in our unconscious access to repressed memories that trigger irrational behavior. However, this auto-reflective movement does not judge, blame or criticize since the Spirit is neutral and curious.

4: A change in the value and priority

Our principles are changed by locating authority within ourselves. Religion has a moral code that is based on a rule structure. "You don't; don't do so." Don't. But now, we can build our ethical framework to assess what is right now. The ego cannot do so because it needs to be guided by essential needs; only the Higher Self can.

This awakening to higher spiritual ideals is why our conduct changes when we wake up spiritually. Maslow called the "being principles" or "b-values" of such spiritual values. They include totality, perfection, fulfillment, fairness, life, elegance, truth, and self-sufficiency.

5: The Inner World Transformation

In the normal waking state of a person, a person's ego concentrates almost entirely on the outside world. All external environmental elements are labor, money, accomplishment, family, friends, and social life.

A big change from this exterior to the inner domain of emotions, feelings, dreams, and imagination is another spiritual awakening symbol. This aspect is called the subtle kingdom in Buddhism, but it is considered more real than our waking state's gross dimension.

6: Holding together opposites

Many of us feel very rigid and fundamentalistic, seeing things in white and black. You're getting the concept from red to blue, democrat, republican, men and women, the right and the right.

We cut off one pair of opposite and associate solely with the other to prevent the uncertainty inherent in adult maturity. For instance, as parents, we may believe that we love our children unconditionally, without recognizing the source of hate and resentment.

And though dissociating ourselves from one pair of things, our self's conflict seems to be resolved, and it just strengthens our shadow. We start holding the stress of opposites within ourselves through our spiritual awakening, leading towards psychic wholeness.

7: Okayness and Inner Freedom experience

The ego is the source of anxiety, desire, and stress. There's an intrinsic feeling of all right if the ego is no longer in control—no matter what happens in our lives. (good or bad).

When the Spirit is at the forefront, we relax instinctively in the outside world, having a sense of inner liberation that we have found once. They call it moksha or self-liberation in Hinduism.

8: Deep self-honesty and personal accountability

You can be radically frank with yourself as you begin to identify more authority within... You can no longer bear the shadow self-disappointment game of Magic.

Now, your feelings, emotions, and acts have an increasing sense of duty and responsibility. That's why David Richo said the last door to mature adulthood was culpable.

There is no transparency when we are unaware of our actions. There is nothing for which to feel bad when there is no responsibility. But the culpability of the spiritual awakening is not shameful for anyone else; it is your conscience motivated by a desire to correct your way of life.

9: A Massive Change in Lifestyle Choices

You become extremely aware of your choices in lifestyle is a noticeable indication of spiritual awakening.

Many "natural" stuff we had previously done is now unacceptable.

When your relation to the planet grows, you start changing your behavior, for example.

Ethics becomes a major driver of comfort.

10: A sense of connectivity or unity

The ego, or the superficial self, as Alan Watts calls it, is separated and alone. They are afraid for their survival and hold on to life as they fear death.

No such apprehension or sense of separation exists in the original Spirit. It's not playing the "us vs." ego game. The Spirit does not associate with sex, race, citizenship, religion, or species. That's just it. And beyond space and time, death isn't a term important to it.

CHAPTER 2: YOU HAVE BEEN SPIRITUALLY AWAKENED

What is your life? What is your life? What's your life's purpose? Why don't you love your whole life? Why are you so afflicted and deprived? Why do you believe that you are valuable and meaningless? Why do you envy the lives of others? Why are you concerned with the views and judgments of other people?

Ok, by saying, "Since you're... not completely spiritually awakened, you should answer these queries." You might think then that you need to be spiritually awakened, profoundly solve these problems, and perfect your life. The truth is not that straightforward.

First and foremost, you were already awakened spiritually. Your consciousness is not open enough to notice the fact, and you have not observed that you were spiritually awakened. So it is the perfect answer to the questions to make your unconsciousness transparent.

You can then wonder how you can clarify your subconsciousness. We can answer the question: have the right awareness and proper practice of your subconsciousness to make your subconsciousness visible. When you feel the selflessness of your subconsciousness or the full convergence with the ultimate subconsciousness (the nirvana), your consciousness becomes transparent and eternal.

You will be your faith and reality naturally in your spiritual development through the right practices to make your subconscious visible. At the end of the process, you will see your spiritual awakening and reality.

Do not be confused between the truth that you can remember your subconsciousness and spiritual awakening when you read this book. The reality is self-sufficiency. This means that you will be the reality if you feel selfless and thus unite the subconscious to the ultimate subconscious. Without selfishness, you are not yourself but the reality. You have immortality as the reality by being selfless.

Spiritual awakening means to see true elements before you are truthful. In other words, it means seeking the right insight and answer about selflessness for your spiritual awakening. All have to wake up to be truthful in mind. Your spiritual awakening is the key to reality! Spiritual enlightenment is not a one-stroke, but the knowledge about reality is gained from inside and above the spiritual moments.

As you can see in the graph above, "Spiritual progress towards Nervana," you can study and practice with us towards truth on four levels. You can call an interconnected stage of spiritual awakenings from level 1 to level 3. Keep in mind that your journey is not over right now! You have the essential degree until you have completely awakened spiritually. Level 4 is all about the reality of the subconsciousness. When we clarify our subconsciousness by studying and practice correctly, we concentrate on spiritual awakenings up to level 3.

Do you believe the truth can be? Naturally! Recall that you were awakened spiritually, and you were the reality too. You had not been selfless for a brief period before you were born. You could feel selflessness all the time, and you couldn't differentiate yourself from others. All were completely unified for you at the time. You couldn't say you had real awareness since these two distinct forms of awareness were the same at the time.

Unfortunately, you were now too well-informed to be the truth. You forgot your spirituality right now. You now experience materialism and false judgments. Working for the truth is simply learning the right awareness and practice to clarify that the subconscious is selfless.

Now, you may wonder how you can show your subconsciousness that selflessness is recognizable. In the beginning, you must learn the correct understanding of your sub-conscience, spiritual upliftment, and selflessness. You will go in the wrong direction without the right understanding, and you will not only never be spiritually saved, but you will never be the reality. With other "seekers" through our services, you will acquire this knowledge.

Second, to strengthen your spirituality and clarify your subconsciousness, you must learn the right practices. You will have the chance to learn the right techniques and practice with us to achieve better results.

Third, by constantly studying and practicing both in your every day and in our programs, you start finding and strengthening your subconsciousness. By having wisdom from the inner and higher selves, you shall discover yourself. The real meaning of your life will be found. You will find in your mind ultimate joy and calm. You will discover eternity by becoming a reality in the absolute awakening of your subconsciousness.

Life's nice, not healthy. You are responsible for making your life very better by focusing on your spirituality if you think your life is healthy. You have now awoken spiritually! Your faith and subconsciousness continue to improve with us. You will find the spiritual development of your subconsciousness in your existence and the everlasting reality of selflessness. Things like financial prosperity, fame, or global happiness, are much greater than anything else.

When we try to come out of bed, the symptoms of a spiritual awakening are close to those of a physical waking.

When we wake up physically, we hit a point where we're not happy to lie just in bed. Simply lying we're tired of. We are told by our bodies to get up. The symbol here is the discomfort we feel in bed. This discomfort drives us gently to wake up.

In a spiritual awakening, we are conscious that the condition of our spiritual life no longer satisfies us. Our mind tells us to go on. This is an indication of spiritual discomfort. Our state of spirituality is not satisfying to us. Our present level of spirituality is to rise above our level.

Secondly, as the light sheds over our eyes by the sun's early rays (if we don't sleep in a room closed to the light in the morning), will trigger our face's nerves so that we can remind ourselves that it is already morning and we need to wake up and work for ourselves. Here is a warning, the first dim light flashing over our heads, but as the morning progresses, it gets lighter.

In a spiritual wake, the light of the Spirit, which brings all other spirits into birth, will shine on our spirits to indicate that it is the morning of our spiritual life already and our work is essential. The sign here is the illumination of the Spirit that falls into our mind and tells us that it is time for us to get up and to do the job that he has assigned.

Thirdly, we wake up during the physical awakening because the rear of our consciousness is already a job to do that day. Normally we think about our job the next day during the night before we sleep. When morning arrives, our mind recalls the work, and we get guided to wake up, whether it is part of our everyday routine or something out of the ordinary routine.

The symbol of a spiritual awakening that we are to awaken spiritually is that our spiritual knowledge tells us that a great deal of work must be done in the world for others. So spiritually, we wake up. We come, as it were, to our spiritual senses.

Fourthly, we are often awakened in physical awakening when there is a risk. Someone shouts that a house has fired or that it has broken down. We are awakened with a strange sound, and we grow to see what this strange sound means. A state of misunderstanding may accompany this.

In a spiritual awakening, someone shouts at our spirits that there is a risk. This scream may come from a priest who tells us that we risk losing our lives; we fall away from the significance of our life. It can come from a book we read silently, reminding us that the world is in great danger. This cry of danger our spirits hear is the warning here. The prevalence of malice around this danger might be. Someone is praying for this, as a way of screaming to heaven, a recognition of sins and failures. Confusion may follow, but the spiritual awakening will lead to enlightenment.

Fifthly, we'll physically wake up in a room with sleeping crowds, like a transport terminal or an emergency center, when we feel another person has already woke up. We won't just wake up the last. We wake up, therefore. We wake up. The symbol is the movement of sleep's first risers.

Others wake up in a spiritual awakening ahead, listening to or reading about it and wanting to wake up spiritually. We are curious about what is happening to others during this spiritual awakening. And we won't be the last spiritually to wake up. The sign here is the spiritual awakening initiative of these pioneers.

Above all, among sociologists and business people, spirituality has become the subject of debate around the world. These emerging trends in culture and the business world do not want to be the last to profit.

Sixth, we can wake up to starvation and thirst in physical awakening. We feel hungry, and we must wake up, get up and prepare for breakfast. The symbol is our sense of physical starvation. It's time to wake up with this feeling. Many who used alcohol last night will feel soaked in the morning. A cup of cold water is what they're looking for, or a round of alcoholic drinks, as alcoholics.

We sense divine hunger or spiritual thirst in a spiritual awakening; our souls are hungrant for the good of life and not only more than the good of this world, such as riches or physical delight. Our minds long for the ideals, which ultimately matter, including lasting love, environmental care, and life's disadvantaged compassion.

Seventhly, when we are on a tour or a field trip on a high mountain, we may want to see the magnificent panorama around us. The first streaks of dawn can hardly wait before we expose the beauty of the plain.

In a spiritual awakening, we could have started an adventure in a spiritual journey and could hardly wait before our eyes for the spirit to unfold. We wake up to see this splendor showing its magic in us spiritually. This symbol is the willingness to ponder in us this spiritual beauty. Through everyone and the whole world, we want to feel our oneness.

Thus the spiritual reawakening is the seven signs:

1) the uncomfortability of the spirit, the dissatisfaction in our state of spirituality

2) the enlightenment of the Spirit who comes upon us enlighten our existence

3) the consciousness of work for other people; not only for our own, the sense of the mission

4) the shouting of a danger heard by our spirits

5) Now, these seven symptoms can be personally or socially learned.

It can be experienced by a single individual, a group of people, or even a whole country. A nation may be so unhappy with its citizens' spiritual condition that people begin to pray spiritually for their awakening. This happened to England in the eighteenth century in the days of George Whitefield and the Wesley Brothers. A prophet will arise and cry out that the nation or the churches are in danger. And then people's pockets hear the yell. It was A. W. Tozer, the 20th-century prophet. Now we profit from this prophet's shouting.

Spiritual awakening takes place throughout us. There are all the signals! Weep for the person who sleeps in these amazing spiritual times.

CHAPTER 3: INDIVIDUAL ALTERATION THROUGH SPIRITUAL AWAKENING

Religious insights provide transcendent illumination. The direction of spiritual awakening is highly sacred, as the illuminated individual interacts with the heavenly and the paranormal. It encompassed various faiths and experiences and was part of diverse cultures and traditions.

Illumination is personal since it suits the knowledge and personal religion of the individual. This means that other people who have not the same opinions can find them different and often disturbing. While many religions have a different knowledge of the Heavenly and Supreme Being, perceptions of spiritual awakening can be similar and unlike.

Different religions and societies share that the spiritual awakening includes the person to break from the sphere and join in several deities and goddesses with God or polytheistic believers. After the awakening, the illumined individual would be deeply connected to the universe. This profound spiritual relationship with the World also allows people and the cosmos to gain intuitive wisdom and understanding.

It is important to keep in mind that this spiritual awakening is not only won by sacred deeds. Living, death encounters, spiritual beginnings, and past life experiences may also achieve the illumined condition. People agitated would claim they had sensual, psychological, emotional, and spiritual fluctuations and problems. Some people have called this creation heavenly, even with its mystery and struggle. This experience is a purely private change, and the awakened will change their activities, habits, and way of life differently.

No one is the same; it must be noted. It is reasonable for each individual to experience his spiritual enlightenment differently. Every person experiences life differently. Let me explain. Let me explain. Some persons with a spiritual awakening can become intolerant to certain foods and allergies. Diverse religions have said it is delicate because the mortal body and intellect are open to the divine and spiritual. This suggests that the body may be less tolerant than before the holy passage and achieve those kinds of things.

Some illuminated persons are more alert and can see auras around living objects. Colors look brighter and also look shut with their eyes at the forms and dazzling colors. They can even hear more sharply than they had before the spiritual awakening. Many people would swear they hear losses when they hear different sounds and find it difficult to recognize different resonances.

Some people's taste, smell, and touch are spiritually awakened. That's why certain people are susceptible to food. Healing times, concluding those memories or something that may have happened in the past could lead to skin rashes at the same time.

The awakened person will experience sudden dominance. Some people claim the heat runs from head to foot, while others say the feeling was elegant and not intense.

It must be noted that the change in a person's spiritual awakening depends on how the gods are seen and understood. We are all different, and not everyone who has attained spiritual enlightenment could have all these personal changes. Whatever your epiphany, hot, cold, food aversion, etc., is your experience, and spiritual awakening is not an erroneous way.

It is not necessary to complicate the journey of spiritual awakening. With an open mental awakening, you will discover and practice the behaviors you experience to become happier.

It would be helped if you tried it all, from yoga breathing exercises to mantra, singing, and all that is between. And you follow these practices when you find practices that help to awaken the divine bliss beyond all creed and ideas. You give it to them with all your heart.

Maybe at first, you don't feel happy when you start practicing meditation; maybe it's complicated, challenge, uneasy. But you may recognize something deep, something very subtle awakening in yourself that attracts you, somewhere in your stay, and that attraction leads to divine happiness.

And if you find ways to bring out God's happiness, you are free to go anywhere. Then your spiritual awakening has opened the door.

If you find it repeating the name of a guru, repeating a mantra, respiration, a certain method of meditation, no matter what it is, if it awakens happiness, then it doesn't matter any of these teachings. All the various philosophies and spiritual discussions are obsolete. Happiness is leading you to a spiritual awakening.

All your concerns and troubles will no longer affect you in the same way if you let yourself slip into this paradise. Since you find a way to awaken divine happiness and this happiness transcends everything. This happiness brings you to something beyond yourself that cannot be expressed in words. It frees you and frees you from your concerns. It's not like when you have a spiritual awakening, and you won't have more concerns and issues. However, you experience yourself outside of it while you are in bliss. You witness a far greater existence, an unlimited, conflict-free reality.

All happens, and it all gets taken care of simply by being in this bliss. It nourishes you and loves you as no one will ever do. God's bliss is clever and knows what to do to lead you to a greater spiritual awakening.

All your concerns and troubles will no longer affect you in the same way if you let yourself slip into this paradise. Since you find a way to awaken divine happiness and this happiness transcends everything. This happiness brings you to something beyond yourself that cannot be expressed in words. It frees you and frees you from your concerns. It's not like when you have a spiritual awakening, and you won't have more concerns and issues. However, you experience yourself outside of it while you are in bliss. You witness a far greater existence, an unlimited, conflict-free reality.

All happens, and it all gets taken care of simply by being in this bliss. It nourishes you and loves you as no one will ever do. God's bliss is clever and knows what to do to lead you to a greater spiritual awakening.

But don't give halfway. Don't give it halfway. Don't focus on a backdoor to go back into questions and intellectual discourse. You will lose your happiness if you allow doubt to creep in. In meditation, you must also be able to release all thoughts. You must not get rid of thinking, and you must stop hanging on to it. You let them go and come.

Don't take the halfway track, don't let the thought and interpretation get lost. Instead, devote yourself to your spiritual practice until nothing remains, even spiritual practice. Even happiness will go.

And then there is just what is; the moment's simplicity. And that's much more enjoyable than happiness. And this is a spiritual awakening.

In obtaining Kundalini Shakti, the illumined vibration of energy provided to you by a lighted guru is the best way to awaken divine happiness. You experience God's bliss by getting this Kundalini Shakti which leads you to the spiritual awakening.

How do I know if I have a spiritual upliftment?

Since spirituality and mysticism are always vaguely wise, the notion of a spiritual awakening can be very confused. One of the most common places to learn of spiritual awakening is Anonymous Alcoholics or any 12-step program.

The 12th and final step indicates that a person can have a spiritual awakening and reach a final state in which his spiritual journey is complete. However, the notion of a "break" of spirituality is troublesome, and we have to be specific about what a spiritual awakening is intended for. Sage people such as Ramana Maharshi, Nisargadatta Maharaj, Lao Tzu, and Sri Aurobindo have addressed these disturbances in greater depth, suggesting they are extremely unusual.

It might better be known that the concept of spiritual "awakening" is that everyone is relative "sleep" in terms of the experience of their everyday life. Often when you're sleeping, you don't even know you're sleeping because your dream can look so true! This is a like perception of the spiritual "sleep."

People who first enter into a spiritual regeneration program or any spiritual community may be said to "sleep" in their knowledge of what is or is most important in their lives. They aim to teach more mature people to "wake up" to the world around them. This can also be very challenging and even traumatic. We particularly don't want to wake up to life more than we would like to wake up when we sleep in our beds from a good dream. However, if we hold on to a spiritual community long enough, we realize these things more, called "waking up" to a new truth.

However, the entire importance of a spiritual awakening is always much more intense than the majority of us know. We had probably had some dreams in the night when we thought we were awake and visited several of the "real" locations, such as work, school, and home. Either we fell asleep without realizing it or just went through another very clear and still surreal dream.

This sense of "dreaming" is also very common in people who start studying spiritual truths and get very excited when they feel "waking up." However, in most instances, it is very far from the fact that this "waking up" is a full-blown spiritual awakening. As a great scientist once said, "You mistake the full light noon for a crack in the mirror!" A spiritual awakening is much deeper and broader than most people know. These interactions are usually confined to a very limited percentage of the population in the past. Many great texts, including the Bhagavad Gita, the Kaballah, and the New Testament, mentioned them.

Some of the world's most remarkable spiritual teachers believe that only one in ten million people can ever be awakened to the full truth of humanity's spiritual state! May that be true? It can be right, for spiritual work takes great commitment and effort over several years before a person can be said to be fully awakened to his or her spirit. Muhammad is believed to have been meditating for years until he becomes "enlightened," and some of the soul's life and death and immortality were deeply affected. You can only be intuited by those who undergo extreme disasters or near-death changes in their lives. Even after these extreme experiences, people frequently return to their original condition and are not fully "awakened" to their spirit but alter only profoundly.

A spiritual awakening is greater than those after hearing the subject were likely to comprehend. The uniqueness of experience, however, can inspire people to dedicate themselves to the same spiritual journey. The experience is very rare. The great spirits contained Muhammad, Teresa's mother, Gandhi, Krishna, St. Paul, Ramanahshi, Gautama Buddha, Lao Tzu, Christ Jesus, and many more names.

An individual can become one of the most important figures in history to search for a spiritual awakening. You will get there one day if you set your course for the stars! There is no more question whether you've arrived or not until you do.

Steps To Spiritual Happiness

Many people believe that spiritual regeneration, spiritual awakening, and a new change of spiritual awareness occur while we speak. If it's a sure sign that the guy was a good camper at the time if you heard a man seemingly in "good spirits."

In essence, every effort we make to raise our spiritual consciousness is meant to make us happier. But you don't have to arrange an appointment with God one by one to learn how to live happier, even though we can profit enormously from this.

Steps to happiness that can be applied to begin today. Certain people will start practicing a little, but each one is easy to add and can quickly change the whole view of life.

1. Caution The Vampire Energy. We all know the sort. Some people have a real crunch, either intentionally or otherwise, to suck others away. Its main subject is to complain about everything, followed closely by criticism and clamor for others. You can sense your joy and mind descending like a single-winged cargo plane if you pay attention. Whenever possible, exclude adverse people from your life and use the other steps mentioned here when you have to deal.

2. Determine what is disappointing to you. The easiest way to figure out what is first is often to classify what it is not. The same is true of happiness. Sit down and write a list of things that you'd rather not do anymore, given a chance. Then you know that you have an option whether or not to continue to do it. When most people sleep, find a 24-hour store and shop. You're going to meet other people of the same mind and even make a new friend. Do you make the TV news frown at night? Stop watching it. Stop watching it. Yes, it's that easy.

3. The Gratitude Attitude. This one we were all guilty of. How much did we see the cup as half vacant rather than half full? We need to be thankful for having a cup. Be very grateful if you have a roof over the head, meals at the table, and two legs with which to walk. Certain

people don't have anything above. If you're lucky to call yourself with your family or friends, please inform them that you're very grateful for your life. You will be happier because you have a kind word in common and you will do your best to make you happy, too.

4. Agreement. A plain acceptance description - this is what it's, and that's all right. A lot of curveballs are thrown into our life. Our happiness or lack of it depends on how we cope with the difficulties. Imagine an ant that demands an elephant to do something. That's what we do when we demand things go our way. Happy people know that both good and bad times will occur in life and that both will have to embrace.

5. Exercise. Researchers at the University of Texas at Austin found that people suffering from depression who exercised on a treadmill for 30 minutes reported feeling more vigorous and had a greater sense of psychological well-being than those who don't exercise. Would you like to be happier? Join a volleyball team, a neighborhood football club, or a backyard family football game. When you combine physical activities and social meetings, you cannot help but feel content.

6. Avoid Judgment. Learn to avoid judging someone when you want to be happy. Learning here is a keyword, and we are all guilty to the extent of that.

Think about how you feel when the slow driver in front of you is silently cursed. Not too fine, perhaps. After all, who of us is perfect? Have you ever gained a way out or unexpectedly remembered that you don't wear matching socks of a restaurant with spinach? We wouldn't feel good about ourselves if someone blamed us for every mistake we have ever made. The negative energy sent out into the world on a spiritual level has been and the decision we ever created. Happy people search for the good of people and stuff.

7. Accept personal liability. We have a right not only to live happily - we also must live happily - if not for our own sake, for others' sake. Our thoughts and behavior influence us and give our children, colleagues, acquaintances, neighbors, and anyone we encounter throughout our lives an impression. We breed more of the same negative of the project. The other way around, too. Happy people are not blamed for their issues for others. You have as much a future as it belongs to anyone else in this country. Take care to make the planet a happy place for everyone you encounter. Remember, there is a large beach even with one grain of sand.

8. Make your life easier. "The rarest thing I know is happiness in smart people." - Hemingway Ernest. Some can make the recipe for ice cubes more complicated. The more we overthink stuff, the bigger it gets, and we get irritated. Make a molehill a

mountain a perfect way to ruin the day. Some of the world's most happy people often own the fewest goods, work, and enjoy simple life things. Many of the places we want to feel comfortable are walking in the Park, a picnic on the beach, or listening to music. 3 Steps To Recovery is an outstanding book describing the incredible spiritual journey of the author and teaching three basic steps to go through. If you are tired, slow down and simplify your life right before leaving for work in the morning.

9. Do any good every day. When we show compassion to others, we feel better about ourselves. You don't have to go to a monastery or become Mother Teresa's next. Keep the next older adult door, stop and let another driver get out of a busy parking lot. Or join your local comfort shop with your smile and a kind word. For those concerned, it becomes a win-win scenario. You have made someone else happy, you're happy, and for everyone, you meet your goodness has also started to wobble. Again, the big beach also has a grain of sand.

10. Live in the current moment. That's my best way to be happy. One of my favorite quotations is from Lao Tzu, a well-known Chinese philosopher. He said you live in the past if you're sad. You live in the future if you're nervous. You live in the moment while you are at peace. The true definition of happiness is inner peace, of course. An incredible thing happens if you

concentrate only on the moment. Step away or even look around you five minutes ago from yesterday and tomorrow. You are here, a tiny but vital part of it all. Take a fountain plumb and understand that the inventor invented this simple tool out of love for his fellow man. For the first time in a very long time, look closely at a flower. Understand that you and the flower were formed by the same divine love source and wonder at the splendor of the soft petals, understanding that although not one human being on earth can produce the flower from scratch, there appear as magic thousands of flowers. Stop and listen to your breath. Know that all is right with you right now, and you can understand the true meaning of spiritual and personal happiness.

CHAPTER 4: SPIRITUAL AWAKENING TAPPING INTO YOUR DESTINY

This section addresses how you can have your spiritual awakening to begin the journey of what you intended to accomplish.

There are several things you need to do with your life to awaken spiritually. The first is not to be linked emotionally to the issues you face today because they concern every thought and, therefore, every decision you make daily. People are in the proverbial rut because they pursue their routines through the years. We don't make any more choices but respond to our environment around us and lead us repeatedly down the same path. Your spiritual awakening, which starts manifesting the things in your life, means something to you, to escape this ruth, which you might want to do.

The Power of Disruption

There must be a type of interruption for any person who uses spiritual awakening. For example, if you go through life as you do every day and unexpectedly have an accident that prevents you from working or even functioning properly, your daily lives will most likely be disturbed. Many people want to understand why the accident took place and what they will do based on their injuries. They will have new habits and experiences once they are recovered, enabling their lives to improve. You will need to be free from your rituals of daily life to have a spiritual awakening. Only then would you be able to walk the way the world has chosen for you in the end. Your interruption may be an epiphany you may one day know or frequently publish utilizing writings. You can no longer bear the life in which you live and are emotionally driven to change this. Therefore, if you want to become the person you want to be, you must disrupt your daily habits regularly, start running from your rut and step on the right way.

Beginning Your New Life

Once you have made a deliberate decision to make a better change in your life and have found a way to disrupt your everyday habits, you can now set your way, assured that you must step on and find a way to make a living and become the person you are to be. Depending on your ultimate goals, this phase can take several weeks or even a few years. In the end, though, you really will achieve spiritual awakening and begin to live the lives of your dreams if you decide to change your life.

You are a busy person, so get your data from a trustworthy source. Quality knowledge about spiritual awakening should be used for your benefit. You found this piece, so take advantage of it.

You need to remember two crucial things whether you want to achieve self-realization or experience a spiritual awakening.

The first step in spiritual awakening is to understand that you are aware of it and dive into it.

Although it's important to realize that you are intellectually conscious, it won't lead to a spiritual awakening. Second, you must understand that you are consciousness itself through self-interrogation or consciousness.

Here are two methods of meditation that will lead you directly to the experience you are aware of.

You keep focusing your mind on yourself in the practice of self-inquiry. You can quietly ask, "Who am I?" or, "What is consciousness?" to help bring your mind back to the past and feel this. At first, you can only feel yourself 1/2 second as a consciousness before you are caught up again. Nevertheless, you will feel more and more conscious by practice.

You encourage thoughts to come, but instead of identifying yourself with them, you witness them. First of all, you encourage thinking to come and go. When they emerge, you deliberately give up thoughts. You don't drive them away and don't keep your emotions passively. You will then reach a point where you will see thoughts emerge and vanish by yourself while you are in your pure state of consciousness. You know that you're wondering, but you're not interested.

These two methods will lead you to the first stage of spiritual awakening, where you know without a doubt directly that you are conscious. That you live as consciousness itself, fully free of mind and body.

In this realization, the second step is to stay. Since emotions are most frequently going to draw you out of this experience. Thus, meditation is the practice of staying for longer periods in this pure state of consciousness until that pure sense of consciousness becomes dominant.

These above practices are ideal for realizing themselves or for spiritual awakening, but they are not complete. There has to be a secondary consideration.

And Shakti is the second factor for a spiritual awakening. Shaktipat is a spiritual force. Shaktipat. You could call it grace; Deeksha might call it. It is the power of pure awareness. In the form of electricity, it is consciousness. And it has the absolute mind to turn you into enlightenment and awaken you. You can feel Shakti as vibration, as happiness, as harmony, love, or energy. But it is the shakti itself, which leads you to self-realization, to spiritual awakening.

You will sense that any part of your body or mind is awakening to unconditional peace and bliss when you receive Shakti.

For Shakti to work, you have to receive Shakti, of which we will speak in a moment, but you must also trust it as soon as you receive it. Through meditation, you encourage Shakti to do her work on your body and mind and experience what you feel. This often entails understanding. You start to get your attention immersed in Shakti's feelings.

Two methods are available for receiving Shakti. The other approach is through an illuminated Guru. You obtain Shakti and quickly achieve deep conditions of meditation and peace by standing in the presence of an illumined Guru.

Sound is the second method. Shakti can be captured and converted into sound through developments in audio recording. So simply by listening to some special music for meditation, you easily achieve deep meditation and natural spiritual awakening. The best thing is that you can get Shakti bliss in your own home or anywhere you go. You need not engage in any particular way or creed structures, and Shakti is on your CD player just by pressing.

Have you previously encountered an Indian Guru or a Buddhist Monk? Many of us never met a human-like that. Everything that we know about is the pictures or interpretations of Hollywood. It's pretty straightforward to assume that they might look dreamy or happy. You may want to do this with a spiritual awakening, but first, you have to divide yourself from the worldly. Many of us live as our main meal in busy towns. It is a life that will rule our lives with deadlines, demands, and high targets. You would most likely want to get rid of these concerns and feelings from time to time, but you will be concerned more with doing this. Can you restore and relieve tension by visiting a resort, playing in your garden, or some other form of peaceful activity? Probably not the answer. It would help instead if you had a spiritual awakening that would heal what you're concerned about.

So what are we talking about this spiritual awakening? A spiritual awakening is a process that helps to balance an individual. It is meant to increase your consciousness, offer illumination, and transcend you into another dimension above all. Is the question now how are you going to get into this condition? Should you be a monk or hermit to focus on your rebornness? It may be helpful for some, but this is a very thorough method.

Spiritual Meditation and Awakening

You need to learn how the mind functions to bring about a spiritual awakening. You must know what concrete, immaterial is and then realize that we are all the results of our minds and processes. There is just a part of our brain where we can perceive things in a certain light before there is a spiritual awakening. We can't count on our interpretation as reality any longer because the mind still filters it and perceives what has been said.

We've heard that the blue is blue, but we can't say it's red and we'd get the same impression? Many who believe in spiritualism are still conscious. Their awakening in the human body believes color to be a delusion because our minds perceive it in a minimal capacity. You have to learn and relax and focus on a spiritual awakening.

Try to picture an unseen dome beyond this dome, which is your mind. It's a place where imagination and emotions can't go. You can find quiet in which your mind is free when you can enter this state. You can experience an all-embracing spirit. Your mind and body will be illuminated, where you keep the truth well and not the false images.

Required practice

Practice is necessary to reach a state of spiritual awakening. You will continue to be peaceful and balanced as long as you can practice.

Steps for Spiritual Recovery

Often it's called a state of illumination. The state of genuine spiritual awakening is a state most people want to acquire. You should take guidelines and measures on the way to spiritual awakening.

Whatever book you are reading or the teacher you are following, do you follow various instructions for achieving spiritual illumination? Several steps include complex meditation, and the spiritual awakening you are searching for ends upcoming. But there are times when people need some direction to reach an awakened spirit. These may be detailed steps or broad ideologies which lead you to your spiritual journey.

Getting organized is a great starting point. It matters not whether you believe in a step-by-step approach or believe that a spiritual awakening only takes place naturally and unplanned. It would help if you truly believed that a meaningful development is possible and must first be recognized. You should look at yourself deeply and discern your shortcomings and challenges – knowing how they relay to you and your world.

You must take the chance to understand the facts as well if you learn more about yourself. Sit in and understand how you contribute to the realm in which you work, considering what you learned about yourself. The attainment of an enlightened spirit is accepting the world's nature and how you react to it.

You have to practice the healing process. Take the path to heal when the questions and issues are remembered. What I mean is not only to concentrate on self-healing but to encourage other people to heal. Self-healing and other people are critical in achieving an awakened state. Another essential element of spiritual awakening is the achievement of equilibrium. The physical mind and body must be fully balanced.

The truth is that we will continue to disagree forever about the innumerable approaches to how to achieve illumination. As long as you have entered that state, you can follow steps for the spiritual awakening. It is also good to have an unwelcome spiritual awakening. The truth is that it doesn't matter what you do now that you've achieved that amount, but rather what you should do now.

Open your eyes and look at your setting. All seems to be in the same condition, or is it? You're, for example, meditating, and you've just finished stretching out your arms and legs. You feel restful, revitalized, well, and satisfied. The session of meditation was fine.

Nonetheless, you often ask yourself for a real spiritual awakening, and I understand it already. Many people will debate how profound and life-changing is the experience of spiritual enlightenment cannot be missed. If you develop spiritually, knowledge of the signs will help you realize that you are already there.

It is not an ongoing thing, and God's awakening will go and come. It will therefore be safer if you know whether or not you are moving closer to it.

Assume that the Buddhist and Christian approaches are our meaning. In this situation, we have a spiritual emergence embedded in the lighting or awakening of consciousness. This conscious awakening is an advanced type of perception that can see the most obvious flesh being passed. This knows, detects, and feels the spiritual growth of his life.

Maybe a solid degree of harmony is one of the more remarkable signs of enlightenment. Individuals who have awakened their minds are more committed to achieving their goals. It seems they have achieved a degree of calmness when awareness, remembrance, problems, and wishes have become unsatisfactory and disruptive. It is like any break you have encountered is set aside and put away, which leads to a straightforward direction between beginning and end.

Self-discipline is among the signs of spiritual growth. After reaching the stage of spiritual awakening, you not only practice your free will but immediately realize which evil things have to be thrown away. Though these acts frequently lead to suffering and provide only passing happiness, people and objects offered by short wishes are no longer entertained.

Self-effacement and love for oneself are both manifestations of an awakened spirit. The desire to learn, understand, and work for the happiness of yourself and others is having the awakened spirit. An awakened spirit would encourage people to start to live with Mother Nature as well as other persons. Empathy and friendship would be equal regardless of community, ethnicity, and nationality.

Sincere bliss, disclosure, correct instincts, and disclosure thoughts are other indicators of a spiritual awakening. Recall that you are looking for some of the above signals after a meditation session. What you discover may surprise you.

CHAPTER 5: HOW IMPORTANT SPIRITUAL AWAKENING

Have you got a tight friendship right now? Have you ever noticed that with every passing day, it becomes more complicated? If you need something like a "spiritual awakening," maybe you as your partner need it. What do you do? What do you do with that? How do I submit to this "spiritual awakening?" Does it contribute to reviving the old fire?

If you are now trying to resolve this tough phase of your marriage, divorce and divorce do not always seem the right option. It would help if you both looked at your accomplishments over the last few years.

Psychologist to Clarify Emotions

Spiritual awakening can be very beneficial for restoring the old link because you were both at the beginning of your marriage. However, couples who have a rocky relationship should first see a marriage counselor or a psychologist before taking such a measure. This must be done to make sure there is no psychotic episode between them. Also, the relationship on both sides can be better understood.

Spiritual Awakening Advisor

Since a counselor can deal only with the couple's feelings, this can't help them correct the issues. This means that a magical, psychological or spiritual adviser is required for you separately. A counselor can help explain feelings and thoughts, but they should require a magical, psychical, and spiritual advisor. The issue is spiritual awakening and paranormal.

The advice these experts provide will help you dig deeper in the bead to assess a person's spiritual needs, the aspect that makes your relationship stressful. This spiritual consultant will do things that can help him to learn what he has suffered from in the past and how the trauma is the source of the present riff.

Even a supernatural, psychic or spiritual consultant has a special capacity to explain the unresolved issues resulting from his divine awakening, former life, or contact from someone else's dimension. This helps you not only to appreciate the experience but also to embrace and understand what is happening to your partner.

If you agree and understand, this means that there is a spiritual awakening between them that is better, as it will allow you to save your relationship, which could be crushed, if you can never. They are easier to be closer with greater sense and sincerity if they fulfill their spiritual needs.

It is important to note that you want a spiritual awakening, but the world around you will always change. This is because you are changing to be different when you achieve a spiritual transformation. And to be better, that means they're going to start allowing more time for thinking and meditation and less time for other mercenary practices.

Spiritual development takes place in several different ways that are special to each individual. But we can refine it into the four things we have to do to bring about spiritual awakening.

Regular practice is the first element in spiritual growth. For most people, the key part of their practice is some meditation. Select and practice a meditation technique every day. It could repeat a mantra silently. It might help you to rest in your feeling of life or consciousness using self-examination or quietly repeating the "I am." It could only be conscious of what's happening now. The most important thing is that the practice works for you enough to last a while.

The second aspect of spiritual growth is your mind and your body. Diet has an enormous significance. What you bring into your body has a big impact on your consciousness and your subtle energy. Exercise is also vital for maintaining a healthy body and helping subtle energy transfer. You are profoundly influenced by what you bring into your mind through TV, music, and other media.

The third reason for spiritual growth, overlooked by many, is the awakening of your subtle energy, also known as the energy Shakti or Kundalini. You sense it as harmony, happiness, or love when this force is awakening in you. Not an impulse, but a very deep thing that draws you. You feel like you are and what it is all about. By obtaining Shakti, you have gained a direct spiritual awakening experience in energy form. This power leads you to a spiritual awakening.

You wake this energy in two main ways. One of them is a direct transmission from an instructor who can pass on Shakti fully illuminated. You will have to travel very far to find and learn Shakti's instructor. Your spiritual growth would go very slowly without that spiritual force.

You begin to wake up to feelings of joy, happiness, love, and quiet when you do these three things, frequent meditation, cares for body and mind, and receive Shakti regularly. Your consciousness will increase, leading to spiritual growth in the fourth aspect.

Spiritual growth and spiritual awakening are the fourth reason to surrender. As you become aware and become more aware of harmony, happiness, love, and silence, you will begin to feel like you are a different "me." For periods, you can experience mental or emotional upheaval, and these times are extremely critical.

And suppose without opposition, you can surrender and only permit that which comes up in consciousness, without any attempts at reform but allow it to be fully accepted. In that case, you are free of yourself and your life's limited vision. You feel like you are a different 'me' and start to settle into unity. You come to know who you are and that you are everything. Spiritual awakening occurs in this realization.

Invoking the spiritual knowledge of the inner soul is spiritual liberation. Many spiritualists have discovered that, even from religious fundamentalists, they can provide or contribute to spiritual development. A degree of spiritual awakening if one feels deeply wise, true to one's inner wisdom, beyond one's mind and impulsiveness in one's heart. The only collector is many petitioners, who did not taste the truth.

The spiritual understanding of the Lord is at the core of every sacred book of various religions and is a true essence of spiritual illumination. But do they have different routines and techniques? Most religions believe that to achieve spiritual liberation, and you clear the conscious mind and logical thinking. Cleanse your mind by fear, attachment, and hatred.

Pure your mind with modesty and compassion. Pure your mind. Purify egoism by following the pilgrimage, prayer, and so forth, without critical thinking and greed. This is not true. This is not true. He trains people's egotism to be illuminated with spiritual wisdom.

The light of spiritual knowledge has no meaning or object. It is now simply latent in your consciousness. Popular perception and touch are not subject to spiritual illumination. He guides you to the wisdom of conscious spiritual development if someone can do this for you.

Many try to get spiritual enlightenment through meditation, fasting, prayer, etc. Along with many, spiritual wisdom has been enlightened. So there is no idea of the wisdom of spiritual awakening, the reach of spiritual wisdom is endless,

To give you an idea of those who claim to have a spiritual awakening or can offer it, obediently follow the symptoms of a charter, the true expert of the spiritual awakening experience.

The expert in spiritual knowledge is always free of its environment like the underwater in the life of the lotus. It absorbs pain, just as the solar system absorbs everything. The expert in the knowledge of spiritual development also extends eternal patience.

Spontaneous as the hot personality of the sun is the pure knowledge character of the real spiritual knowledge of the law. The authority on wisdom in spiritual development is purified as impurities cannot penetrate water's purity. The spiritual awakening specialist knowledge lights up like the skylights upon the earth. The spiritual expert equals the enemy and comrade and has no ego.

The spiritual knowledge specialist is happy in all things, always impartial and the nectar of pureness. There is no technical need for awareness of spiritual growers. He is still correct and warning. He is still right. He loves the closeness of the echo of calmness. The real spiritual wisdom of every rule is still in its state of mind. I'm also looking for spiritual awakening experts who welcome him with dignity.

Explore Your Spiritual Side

I recommend that you explore your spiritual side to achieve full completion in life!

It is also necessary to cultivate and explore your spirituality while taking care of your physical health. As human beings, we can learn and understand in great depth. We will lack a deep sense of fulfillment and inner peace if we do not pursue those possibilities in our absence.

It is good to have the conviction that there is a reason and meaning for life to grow entirely as human beings, that life is part of a whole in which we belong and that there is a force (I believe in God) that can sustain us; in times of need!

There is a sense of fulfillment and integrity, which comes with the quest for spiritual knowledge in whatever form it takes, which enriches and lifts us beyond everyday life!

Many people prefer to bypass this area, aside from the practical and material demands of life today, especially in the West. But it is very easy to cultivate the spiritual side and can only encourage and promote an occupied way of life. We are flat, missing the real objective, and life can be harsh without this spiritual dimension.

When one takes an interest in spirituality, several paths can be taken, and in general, they all lead to a sense of peace and fulfillment. Peace is to be chased, particularly internal peace, because you can carry it to others if you find it.

You have to learn and discover how you find your inner peace!

It is a question of how the soul is at one with its conditions and environment and where it is at one time. You can stroll along a beautiful beach with a gorgeous sunset or spend time in an area where you have experienced peace and love.

You can find this peace by worshiping in a local church or by private meditation or spiritual means. The path of spiritual discipline can be daunting and exciting by disciplining yourself physically and mentally.

It is important to know who you are, why you do what you do and what you want to do with the rest of your life to begin your spiritual journey. You will increase harmony and understanding, health, and well-being by building your spiritual face.

With a spiritual awakening and realization, you can forgive yourself for the sins of the past and allow you to better understand your life journey.

Explore your spiritual side is essential, so start today!

You will find peace at some time, and soon when you persecute it, start or continue your journey and trust!

CHAPTER 6: TO HELP YOU ACQUIRE SPIRITUAL WISDOM AND SPIRITUAL AWAKENING

At the first stage of spiritual growth, an individual begins to think about the world's scholars and spiritual leaders? What are your moral obligation to his family, society, the world, and other ways of life? In the first step of spiritual awakening, a practical person will be free from malice and be freely attached and egoistic.

He realized the unity of the creation of the earth as a spiritual core of right actions and spiritual growth with the ultimate goal of union with God as an individual in spiritual awakening. At this point, the individual understands that all of them will be assessed to achieve spiritual development through their acts and performance.

In his desire for good Karma thoughts, he saw active physical life and manages the natural way of life, the spiritual right to awaken the knowledge of the Interior. This allows the taste of various kinds of wishes for different subjects and things in your subconscious mind. Wishing choices, which are endorsed by divine karma, control the life cycle. This is the first stage of spiritual awakening when a man starts thinking ahead of spiritual development in this world?

How do people live happily? Is spiritual development considered? How will the spiritual knowledge of inner life be awakened? The one who raised the notion of moral obligation, human rights activist and conscious that thought is an ongoing process.

The second stage of a spiritual awakening is an authentic person with the spiritual awakening of the inner spiritual knowledge that the thinking process is ongoing. With the wisdom of thinking, the inner reality of the spiritual awakening is not known! With the knowledge of the technique, a real person who knows the many ways of structure and elegance that colored dresses are made and decorated!

This view takes into account the spiritual essence of physical existence in various ways!

The spiritual wisdom of the inner world, the number of characters, and many lessons to remember! Through the spiritual wisdom of within, many prophets of the sun have become aware of it. Each world and the earth are created! With the wisdom of many inmates, who are mindful of Buddha's reality, yoga teachers and many of God's followers are shapeless.

The mind of many true angels and devils, many philosophers, and the solitude of the seas are many gems with the spiritual knowledge of the interior. Assessment of the interior spiritual wisdom has no consciousness limits! It is truly boundless.

A pious individual is the third stage of spiritual awakening, being a strong spiritual modesty to understand the language. This man is lovely, pure, and pious! In the deep silence of mind and conscience, the devoted individual is always absorbed. The spiritual individual who listens in a pure language of silence is absorbed and believes in pure knowledge of the forms without form and love for God.

It's an incredible beauty to come early on in physical life, and it's awesome! Everybody singing the silence of the pure consciousness in the field of modesty cannot express it in words. In a language of silence, we may speak wisdom, insight, and experience of peace.

In the third stage of spiritual awakening, the language of physical life is the pure expression of conscience that lacks avarice, terror, attachment, and vanity, the memory of mind, conscience, and consciousness. All have a samadhi experience! A human being with modesty conscious of the infinite and subtle produced the universe and can be checked for his existence. An individual with a sense of humility agrees to live with the silence that sings of pure knowledge and pure love that is aware of the skeleton of God in formlessness;

A religious individual who becomes strong in the spiritual awakening life cycle is the fourth and final stage of spiritual awakening. Here the spiritually enlightened person is completely imbued with the spiritual silence singing in the knowledge of karma. Silence means silence singing to silence the mechanism of mind, freedom of expression, and freedom of conscience.

This stage of spiritual awakening is pure nectar of the pureness of the karma sphere, knowing that the accounts of karma are to remain alive! The pure, spiritually illuminated mode of life here is entirely spiritual of God's heart.

Here is an abundance of the duality of action and reaction that is eternal in all its glorious glory! The beauty of the pureness of the immortal nature of life cannot be represented in a language which is the earth's sound in the fourth stage of spiritual awakening! In the fourth phase of the spiritual awakening, many people live unformed in God in many facets of their lives in the world! They keep drinking the nectar of God's pureness to begin their everlasting mortal! A true disciple of God saw the pure form of life with no gladness, but the nectar of his conscience remained saturated;

Rip Van Winkle, do you remember? Those who passed high school years in the 1950s to the 1970s recall him in America's English-speaking part of the country. He was the guy who had been sleeping in New York City for 20 years.

A short overview is available to the younger generation who doesn't know much about Rip Van Winkle. In Washington's story "Rip Van Winkle," he was the main character. He was a Netherlander American who didn't want a charge to function. He just wanted to play. He just wanted to play. One day, as it was before the American Revolution, he was lost in the mountains in New York and was joined with his fantasies and the team of Henry Hudson. He drank and slept. He drank their drink. After just 20 years, he woke up with a long beard and an older adult. He goes back to his village to find that he didn't leave it anymore. Now America has become independent of the UK. He found his family after searching.

I began with the story about Rip Van Winkle because he showed the person who is sleeping in his body for many years, who is only awakened after many years of sleep.

Like Rip Van Winkle, most people sleep in spiritual life, and if anyone wakes, you can continue to sleep spiritually, maybe for the rest of your life. Some of them are just going to wake up forever.

There are three different ways to understand that you had a spiritual awakening. If you're still sleeping, that's psychologically like Rip Van Winkle mentally, and it is time for you to wake up. You have not been through these two forms.

And that's the difference from physical awakening to spiritual awakening. You can't tell if you are dreaming if you're physically awake. You can't know that when you sleep, you're awake. But you know you're still not spiritually awakened. How does this happen? If you think about your life, whether there are any of these directions in your life! If they're not, that means you haven't been spiritually awakened yet. You will now wish to be spiritually awake if you know this. And to be spiritually awakened is the phase before being spiritually awakened.

Happily, how we feel that we have had a spiritual awakening is close to how we have experienced a physical awakening.

The first way to realize you're physically awake is to become more conscious of your surroundings, first indistinctly, then little by little.

You will tell even before your eyes open that you are awake, still in bed, late in the night or early in the morning, etc.

Yet, you know the spiritual realities surrounding you in your spiritual awakening. You know you are in both a spiritual and a physical universe. Again like during the physical awakening, this consciousness is initially indistinguishable, yet with time this awareness becomes clearer and clearer as you continue through our spiritual path.

This knowledge of your spiritual reality will result in your frustration with your current work, your business failure, your loved one's loss, your joyful meetings with a lover. Whatever this consciousness causes, you are conscious of the spiritual and non-visual things around you, such as love or terror, inner peace or chaos, excitement or uncertainty. You are not just real, visible things.

Did you feel this? If you did, you started to awaken spiritually.

Physical awakening means opening your eyes and seeing things around you: the fading darkness or sunshine, the furniture around the bed, the light shutter, the doors,... after you have become conscious of your natural environment.

Thus you, too, open up your spiritual eyes in spiritual awakening and understand the spiritual realities around you: the efforts of humans to better their lives and achieve ultimate happiness, the crimes committed in the quest for some fulfillment, the exultation and the happiness of those who succeed, the struggle between good and evil that happens before your very eye.

Are you aware of these spiritual realities? Do you see the mighty spiritual powers calling for your attention under the stories of sordid crimes and conflicts, of natural and human disasters? Do you see the growing crowds of people deeper into poverty and homelessness? Are you aware of the few elite leaders in this world who want to purchase resources and only waste them beyond their consumption? And do you view these events as part of a spiritual war, beyond psychological, sociological, economic, and political considerations between the universe's unseen good and evil powers? See the forces behind our world leaders that drive them to rule and manipulate people? You had a spiritual awakening if you did.

Third, you get out of bed, go to the toilet... and so forth to prepare for the work of the day. Thirdly, once you become conscious and have opened your eyes, you act. You get out of bed.

In a spiritual awakening, you will be involved after being conscious of your spiritual environment and have seen what is spiritually happening around you and the world. You brace yourself for your spiritual practice. You don't fall in helpless resignation because of the huge spiritual powers surrounding you, and you believe you can do nothing. You act because you are persuaded that your Spirit is more powerful than your thousands of problems.

You're doing it, but you're not reckless. You are not unprepared for battle. So you put on the shield and the arms of a spiritual nature in spiritual warfare, fully ready to defeat your opponents.

Are you struggling to make this planet a better place to live in, even in your corner of the world? If you say yes, you behave, and spiritually you're awake.

The three ways you can tell if you have had a spiritual awakening:

1. The spiritual realities around you are conscious of.
2. You are opening your spiritual eyes to spiritual powers around you.
3. You are spiritually behaving in your corner of the world to make it a better place to live.

If you do, you know that you are awake spiritually and can inspire other people to wake up spiritually now.

Millions of Van Winkles Spiritual Rip around you have been sleeping spiritually for years, decades. It is your job as a spiritually awakened person to help you spiritually awake.

CHAPTER 7: AWESOME SPIRITUAL AWAKENING SYMPTOMS

The quest starts whenever the soul wakes up, and you will never return. From then on, you are inflamed with a peculiar longing that will never remain in the lowlands of self-sufficiency and partial satisfaction. You are urgent by the eternal. You are disgusting to allow compromise or risk to stop you from fighting for fulfillment. You are disgusting. ~O'Donohue John

For those of you who do not know what a spiritual awakening is, the process is that the person is conscious of the spiritual nature of the whole physical reality and the spiritual nature.

An individual passing through a spiritual awakening realizes that people are so much more than just their name, profession, status of connection and possessions, immortal spirits bound to each other, the earth, and the whole cosmos.

Biologically, we are all related. The universe of chemistry. The rest of the world atomically." Tyson Night Night

We wake up to life literally as we experience a spiritual elevation. We begin to challenge everything, including our old beliefs, conduct, and morals and know that life and ourselves have a lot more to do than we have been taught up to this day.

A spiritual awakening typically involves a variety of incredible symptoms that I will document below. Since each person is special, and every perspective is subjective, not everyone is experiencing precisely the same symptoms in the spiritual awakening.

The following list is based on the symptoms I experienced in my spiritual awakening.

Symptoms of Spiritual Evocation

1 - Reduced stress and exaggeration

Suppose a person knows that they are so much more than their physical shape, their perspective changes. We seem to become less emotionally active in all the things that happen when we put our ego under our control and the spirit inside us; we are less serious.

Problems and unpleasant circumstances that occur can be viewed more critically or, as I would say, "from the viewpoint of the third person" and can be easily resolved and overcome.

Everything in this physical world can eventually be seen as impermanent and meaningless, so why distress it?

2 - Feeling like you were a different person

Some day you wake up and look back one year and realize you are extremely distant and separate, while you are familiar with who you used to be.

As I recall, I remember that I used to feel like a confused, lost child; a child who was not only ignorant but as far removed as possible from the path to clarity.

Even though I can't believe the transition, I've been exposed to it one year later. I still feel puzzled about different circumstances, but confused... I'd like to be puzzled about situations.

As important as before, external stimuli do not matter. People from whom I used to clung seem to isolate me naturally, and I hold my distance. Situations that brought me joy seemed more and more hollow and pointless. I seem to enjoy the time I spend by myself and sometimes even feel I need it.

None of this seems to matter as long as I continue on the journey to know myself.

Finally, the route is defined and more visible than ever.

3 - Increased open-mindedness

We have been taught to live our lives in certain ways since our younger age; those around us completely influenced us.

When the spirit inside wakes up, we are more and more able to understand that almost everything we have been told about life is false and obsolete. It seems almost like we have to bear a very heavyweight, a heavyweight.

However, however frightful and uncomfortable the reality is, we have no choice but to drop that dead weight and expose ourselves to this new state of being to preserve our sanity and strength to move forward.

If we begin questioning everything, our mind eventually opens to a whole new way of being, and it remains forever open. This makes it much easier for us to get out of our comfort zones, look forward to new experiences, enjoy new people, see new places and learn about different cultures. To extend our horizons even further.

A modern mind will never return to the old dimensions of a new experience. Wendell Holmes, Jr. ~ Oliver Holmes.

4 – Intense Clarity, Serenity and Bliss experience

The intrinsic attributes of our Authentic Spiritual Selves are clarity, serenity, and bliss. They are not qualities that can be cultivated but qualities that come to light as our true spiritual nature is clearer, and conditions begin to peel off.

The more we become conscious of and interact with the spiritual essence of reality, the more insight, calmness, and happiness we can experience.

5 - Spontaneous Bursts of Creativity

As awareness rises to higher dimensions, and mental models begin to diminish or even disappear, becoming subtler. We can think further out of the box and see the larger picture.

Often unforeseen bursts of imagination will allow us to make tremendous progress in addressing the issues we currently face, find solutions to previously complex and unanswered questions, and eventually understand who we are really and why we are here, maybe even the meaning of our existence.

6 - Stability of Emotions

Awakening, like being on an emotional roller coaster, extreme mood changes, abrupt emotional waves, emotional confusion, hopelessness, sole, and unconnectedness, are some of the signs that most individuals, places, and books tell you are spiritually awake.

Although this may be the case, these feelings are just like waves on the ocean's surface. There may be a storm over the ocean showing big waves, but the more deeply you dive into it, the calmer the storm appears.

As the Spirit within wakes and we immerse ourselves more deeply in our true nature, we realize that regardless of the emotion that causes turmoil on the surface, there is still this deep ocean-like peace.

7 - Oneness Experiencing

Unity is most likely the most incredible and singular expression of a spiritual awakening.

However, though I am about unity, I will not understand the infinite relation between all and Self in the Universe. I am rather talking about realizing the unity of opposites or the principle of polarity that the alchemists and hermeticians call it in The Kybalion.

The two are the same, and the two are different; the pole is the same; the opposite is the same, but the opposites in degree are different; the extremes meet; every truth is an only half-truth; all paradoxes are reconciled.

In every loss, there is victory. The basis of happiness is sorrow. Anxiety brings calmness. Courage comes out of anxiety. Courage. Failure is a success story. The response is the same as the issue arises.

Everything we consider as negative is unmistakably optimistic. Without positive, negative cannot exist, and positive cannot exist without negative.

More significant than the note itself is the silence that arises from each note. It's the vacant space between the notes that makes music actually music. There is only constant sound if there is no void. Changing your thoughts by Dr. Wayne W. Dyer – Change your life

When the awakened man realizes this, he is still in charge of the good in every bad thing, and thus continually. He is still focused, even during chaos; he is not swung, even in luxury; he is in contact with his root.

8 - Life moving more easily

During a spiritual awakening, we become aware of the direct use of our belief system, emotions, and mental states in our lives. In our lives, everything we think appears to unfold.

This understanding enables us to stand at the door of our mind and understand bad habits while dropping everything we think we can stop being the best version of ourselves.

After that, we begin to manifest our wishes more quickly and effortlessly; everything seems to fall into place. Problems alone seem to be solving.

More like a video, life sounds.

9 - Craving Our True Objective

We prefer to discover ways of gratifying our senses when in the state of ignorance of our Spiritual existence We think this is the only path to true and permanent happiness, so we continually set materialistic objectives. We "must" do something, we "must" meet more people, we "must" fall in love, we "must" have money for it.

Battlestar Galactica: There's never enough, you know. As Gaius Baltar insightfully says. Not enough money, business glory. Never enough money. The more desired you like, the more desirable. More money, more fame, and more people are still hungry. The argument we lack is that the focus of your whole life is certain futility that tries to fulfill appetites that can honestly never be sat down. Gaius Baltar - Galactic Star

Now we are awake, and hopefully, we can sense that none of these shallow wishes will make us very happy and peaceful. The only means of achieving happiness are looking past the physical shape and physical shape.

Everyone on earth has been born to fulfill a mission, and while every person has a different goal to accomplish, we all have the same goal of living our own lives and becoming our most Authentic Selves.

Spiritual awakening is an event involving a perception of a holy dimension of life to which you belong. Brainwave training is a technique you can use to speed up the spiritual awakening process by changing your brain wave frequency to resonate in the region of your brain, which triggers an increase in your consciousness, which finally links you with All-That-is or with the Divine.

The moment you experience a Union with God happens in the Awakening.

This is when we realize that we are an immortal spirit, part of the artistic group and part of the Divine.

Awakening exposes the core of your life, taking you beyond this realm of physics.

· Most people have a gradual process of awakening, which takes months or years to complete.

· Awakening can come from disgusting experiences such as physical or emotional trauma, such as losing someone or experiencing your own near-death experience. Often an awakening is a single incident that instantly changes your life. You never forgot it, and all your life, you are referring to the moment as it came from a deep, strong state of consciousness. Spiritual awakening is often a gentle process that develops after years of spiritual self-development.

· The wind may knock most of your spiritual awakenings out, particularly when the Kundalini begins to rise. It is rare at once, as there is normally heavy suffering. · · Intense emotions, anxieties, or fears may open a vortex into which you are drawn. When this happens, you are pulled into the force of the consciousness of the Creator that supports and reassures you. From here, in its purest state of consciousness or presence, you witness your true self.

If you decide to do so, the path to awakening can be speeded.

Ten Spiritual Awakening Signs

Spiritual awakening, also known as spiritual illumination, is an awesome journey to take in brainwave training. This technology is established scientifically, alters your brainwave frequency, and changes your consciousness to the desired state to help you progress faster.

Spiritual awakening is an event that involves realizing or opening to a frightening dimension of reality that lasts your life. It can be called an experience of mysticism, near death, liberation, or illumination of your consciousness.

Spiritual Awakening Signs

1. Scent, touch, taste, sound, and sights enhance the five senses. Your food taste has improved. Chemical additives that turn you off can be detected. You will be pleased with the scent of the flowers and distracted by it. Without the radio, you can begin driving, realizing that your environment is already too much noise. The green of the leaves appears almost neon in the spring, and they fascinate you. You have almost abrasive fragrances that you enjoyed before.

2. Periods that keep you going intensely. After cycles of tiredness and lethargy. Roll with energy and be

gentle to yourself. Take a nap when you're tired. Take advantage and make the energy if you want to jump up and reorganize your room or paint a frame.

3. A tingling, scratching, and creeping feeling in the scalp. A sense of energy vibrates over your head as your chakra of the crown opens. You exchange details with mutual unwillingness when you open your crown chakra.

4. The sleep pattern changes. When you go to sleep, your feet can feel warm or tingling. You are still, and you wake up during the night several times. Now is a good time to think about the rest of your brainwave training. Training sessions can be compared to daily sleep for 4 to 6 hours.

5. Emotional are you. Nothing is wrong, particularly if you have tried not to do it before. It does not matter. Accept your thoughts as they are coming and going. You begin to purify your emotional condition.

6. The weight changes. 6. When your feelings are being healed and handled, your humanity feels that you need to defend yourself and eat to guard. That's not going to get out.

7. You feel the need to handle past events. Suddenly, you feel like you have to deal with problems that you have smothered with. You feel like you've got your feelings right back in the moment, and this time.

8. You have a food allergy that never has affected you. When you spiritually wake up, you become more sensitive to everything around you, including everything you eat. Your body now clearly communicates food and can tolerate it or not. Your body starts to clear and purify toxins. When you wake up in the morning, you can have white stuff at the corners of your mouth.

9. What you want to eat changes. You may have food cravings that you have never been aware of before. You can feel hungry or hungry less than normal.

10. Bump and rashes eruptions. Your feelings carry it to the surface, so the rash, bumps, acne, hives, and shingles appear on your skin. The mouth and the chin show up with color. These bumps remain until you tackle something that has made you feel.

You will speed up the process and feel symptoms if you wake up to your spiritual brainwave training. Speeding your path would take you further so that you will profit faster from a spiritual awakening. Spiritual awakening will take years of strengthening of symptoms without the use of training.

Unless you process your things, a spiritual awakening cannot happen.

And the most illuminated spiritual doctors will find it difficult to translate a spiritual awakening into words.

Although many of us come across ordinary encounters at some stage, they do not necessarily point to spiritual awakening.

Many people will confer any otherworldly experience as a manifestation of spiritual awakening, correctly or wrongly, if you leave. Many consider being so profoundly meditative and mystical influenced by inner harmony construed to describe spiritual realms.

Many who have been on the road to spiritual awakening will admit that this is a long and necessary journey and every small step along the way. A vast array of euphoric experiences, whether surreal to the divine, will manifest as one progresses to spiritual Gyan or spiritual awareness.

It is extremely pleasing to experience such wide emotional dimensions and stays in mind for a long time. The mind's tendency to recap and revive this transcendence coaxes the mind into outside notions of spiritual awakening and illumination.

CHAPTER 8: SPIRITUAL AWAKENING AND A TRANSFORMATIONAL SHIFT IN CONSCIOUSNESS

There's a spiritual change. No doubt about there. It's no doubt. In the breeze, you can nearly sense it. There seems to be a lot of people around the world on the brink of gigantic stuff. Although their interactions cannot always be explained rationally, something unprecedented certainly takes place.

In recent decades millions of people worldwide have witnessed a profound and unlimited openness to their true existence. There are somewhat unmatched reports that there are upwards of 15 million people in the world now who fit in with this definition of "spiritual emergence." Still, the figures that you are calculating awareness are not substantial.

Moreover, as a critic mass of "wakened" people reside on the Planet Earth, a so-called "tipping point" occurs and lifts all of us into a more aware, enhanced consciousness and eventually a constant awakening experience. People worldwide speak about how they become sensitive to new approaches, industry, or changing perceptions and social values. We also note how they view their lives and experiences individually in a very different way. Every day, paradigms change. It cannot feel easy to maintain.

In due course, these changes probably lead to a complete awakening experience, but nobody can know all of these days! All we have to do is to witness and record the past testimonies of those who seem to have woken and registered them naturally over the last few years. The reassuring thing is that their testimonies seem to confirm one another.

Some people help to make it happen, others are watching it happen, for some people it happens, and some people are wondering with their hearts in their mouth, "what is happening on earth, without having to sound flippant?" In reality, many people cannot understand what they're doing and feel pretty darn uncertain and even afraid of what lies ahead. There are abundantly pessimistic 2012 forecasts, and although widely misunderstood, some people fear the end of the world is at hand - it is actually!

Many 'doomy and dim merchants' claim that this time is about the disintegration and disintegration of all the systems that we make, the end of this planet as we know it: a gigantic, karmic rebound that is bouncing back on humanity and anything that we have created is systemically removed that does not support us as a species or aligned with Reality. This could be legitimate in certain respects because an outage would eventually occur in advance of renewal. However, this is a moment of global initiation. We like to believe: a golden age, spoken about by visionaries and mystics for the ages - when humanity will eventually grow into collective waking.

What if the various reasonable possibilities were available? Perhaps this is a moment where we are all challenging the divide we have built between mass in consciousness and awakening to our true nature and our full participation in the universe.

In the first place, this era of transformation looks like a time when we look at the division between worldly accomplishment and awakening to our True Selves, which is systematically manifested in our external creations and experiences. "Out there is not the world."

Learn why you feel so unbalanced

The incredible energetic phenomenon of 'waking up' keeps gaining pace and strength and affects more and more people. This is only an indication of the interactions that it can lead to. In reality, we have seen many of them for years, so it's nice to know that a reasonable explanation exists! We can relate to most, if not all, of the symptoms. We advise that this not be overthought; the grain of awakening is too analyzed.

People love to visit medical sites and forums, associate their symptoms with life-threatening illnesses and wildlife. Please check this list as a reference framework in the spirit in which we share it. However, if you have any real physical health conditions, please contact a physician.

Geoffrey Hoppe of Crimson Circle, who channels Tobias, was influenced by the following.

Spiritual Awakening Signs

1. The body, particularly the neck, shoulder, and back, suffer and pains. This is the product of intense changes at the level of your DNA as the "Christ seed" awakens. That's going to happen.

2. No clear explanation for feelings of deep inner tranquillity. You release your past (this and other lives), which causes sorrow. This is like the experience when you have lived in a new house for several years. There is a sorrow to leave memories, energies, and experiences behind the old home, as much as you want to drive into the new house. This is going to happen in time.

3. No obvious reason to cry. The above is the #2. The tears are good and good safe to allow the old energy to flow. This will occur on waves and will also occur with the release of the old energy.

4. Your work/career changes suddenly. This symptom is very normal. Things around you are going to change when you change. Don't think now about "great"

employment or career. You are in transition, and before you settle into one that matches your passion, you will make some adjustments.

5. Nothing enthusiastic or enthusiastic. The feeling that nothing excites you is related to the above symptom. You don't echo the old passions anymore, but you haven't developed the new. You can feel bored sometimes. Stick tightly, and over time it will adjust. We have upgraded our DNA and internal applications, meaning that our old reference points are no longer reliable.

5. Family & friends drifting away. You are related through old karma to your organic family. When you get out of the karmic loop, the links between the old ties are freed. It seems like your family and friends are moving abroad. Over time, if you feel correct, you can even develop new relationships with them.

6. Extraordinary sleep habits & sleep disorders. Between 2:00 and 4:00 AM, you will probably wake up several times. A lot of work takes place in you, and you sometimes wake up to a "breath." Don't think about that. Don't worry. If you can't fall asleep, stand back and do something instead of staying in bed, stress your sleep shortage!

7. Loud and lucid dreams. Any of your dreams can be very vivid and maybe like a hunt, war, or dreams like monsters. Once again, you release old energies, mostly

symbolized as wars, chased, or struggling with terrible monsters. They are stored. That's going to happen in time.

8. Feeling disoriented physically. Many people suffer from times of dizziness or feel unfounded. You begin to walk between 2 worlds, so it makes sense that you often feel challenged spatially. You often move into the new force, but your body lags. Time in nature can help build up the new energy inside (ideally barefoot).

9. More to talk to you. There is a new stage of communication in your being, the beginning of this new kind of self-talk. As discussions develop, fluency, consistency, and, most interestingly, perspective will become increasing. You don't go insane; you wake up!

10. Feeling alone, even though others are around. This relates to above paragraph #5. It is a challenge for many of us to be around others who also release energy from the previous era. Some people claim that it's because our Guides, who were with us throughout our lives, have gone to fill our place with our divinity. Early enough, the love and energy of your own higher consciousness will fill this vacuum.

12. Would like to leave the world. All of us have a strong and profound urge to go home. This differs greatly from suicide and does not rely on anger, depression, or rage. You either don't tell anyone about it or don't probably understand it because you don't

want to generate drama. You finished your karmic cycle and feel restless and lonely. You will soon begin interacting with other like-minded persons, and there will be new interests and passions. You have come so far, so do not check out now in the new energy before the next stage of the journey happens. We live in the moment of great change in the most exciting time ever.

You're never alone, and many people feel like you're alone. Connect with someone who has the same mind and take the time to learn more about yourself. Feel in what's singing your heart.

Spirit knowledge Do you live in a position of consciousness? Those that have previously been significantly uncommon, so we try to ease some of your worries, bring your experiences into perspective, and help you make sense of what you find in all aspects of your everyday life, and show you how you can apply spiritual concepts to them all.

You can nurture your mind by practices such as meditation, religious singing, or something so simple that transforms your everyday life into an aesthetically pleasant, sacred, and contemplative space.

Physical activities such as meditation, martial arts, dance, and respiration will help you anchor the divine's awareness in your body and give you the energy for a spiritual journey empowered and passionate.

Spiritual activities for the mind include:

- Meditation.
- Reading spiritual texts and reflection every day.
- Helping you clear up the emotional and mental disruption that prevents us from experiencing inner liberation and leads us to know the universe more personally and with joy.

Bringing more knowledge and awareness to all aspects of our lives will only help raise and catalyze all around us by osmosis! When you view life from the spiritual viewpoint, it is easier for you to treat your body, mind, and soul with reverence and affection – as a temple of the sacred and a gift of the universe that brought you alive at this very moment in this world. We wish you no less and eventually all of humanity. We wish you no less.

Then, what does Awakening mean to us? It is a term you have heard in mystical circles thrown around, often used as a New Age parallel to Eastern ideas of illumination. However, this name is being used more often nowadays, even in more conventional circles like the everyday media, yet it remains surrounded by a lot of charisma (and fear).

· What does it mean in practice?

· How do you wake up?

· How can I tell if there has been an awakening?

We can't tell you because we're not completely awakened. Nevertheless, both of us will experience the vibrational changes in ourselves and wait and watch with curiosity and excitement! We also experience some strange and wonderful emotional and physical manifestations, which seem to connect to contemporary stories about "signs of awakening."

Q. How do you know if you've had an Awakening?

A. Well, like an orgasm, you don't have to wonder whether you had one.

You might consider awakening as a "different consciousness" experience.

Most people live in a state of profound mental engagement and identity with our thoughts and feelings every day. We may not realize that we are not minded or pay less attention to his sometimes destructive conversation. When we experience things during the day, we feel sensations in the body, watching nature and people come and go and still hear the sounds. We are, however, involved in the "actual" world. Our focus is more dedicated to our emotions, concepts, perceptions, and projections of our experiences from the past and present than to the moment itself.

Very few people can be 100% present or know what it means to be present. Most of the world has no idea that you can even choose your thoughts, let alone watch them calmly and without feeling as they float over their mind's surface. If we understand this and start to practice 'watching' the thoughts and cleaning out our obsession with our identity, who and what we are is exposed, as we gradually strip who we are not — just like peeling back the layers of an onion.

Increasing the Spirit Move to the heart and trance

When we awaken, it seems that we realize the harmful twists and turns of the majority of our minds (such as being aware of a TV show in an alien language in another place that does not engage our entire attention).

It is important to know that while it is not possible to control the thinking which flows in our minds, we can control which thoughts we choose to follow. We can start to attract similar thoughts with similar energy in as little as 17 seconds. The 17-second rule, both positive and negative, is applicable and forms the basis of the Law of Attraction. We draw more attention and attention to what we want.

Thus, you call for more such thoughts into your experience if you run a negative scenario over and over in your mind. You are preparing for this journey and laying it before you.

The first step to changing this trend is to capture yourself and change the thinking intentionally. Think of something better, more inspiring, and concentrate on this thinking for at least 17 seconds to create a more optimistic stream of thought.

When we can change attention from thinking about life and our issues to being present in every moment and encounter this moment in our presence, we become new and open to everything around us, rather than reactive and working from past conditioning and the usual frame of reference.

Another perfect way to transition from negative emotions to more empowering and uplifting feelings in the heart is to take three deep conscious breaths that feel the energy moving through the body.

In a breath and then spreading through my body and starting from my hands and feet, I like to imagine golden energy.

Much of our subconscious behaviors are lifetime patterns of thinking, emotions, and actions... before we decide whether to be fresh, inspiring, or, ultimately, to find out how to remain brand new and open to something with little or no thinking.

Remember, a belief is just a feeling that we keep thinking - change your thinking.

Our spirit, our intuition, tells us that the way to live is instinctive. We long to witness our lives directly and be completely aware of what is nowhere. Awakening is ready to change to what is possible and to wake up from the trance of the mind and turn up constantly and refreshed with what is there at the moment.

More and more people are looking for methods for integrating awakening consciousness into their daily life.

How can you live from a place of consciousness, which is current to the present? How can you turn your mind into 'no mind'? How can your lives transition to a fresher, more urgent connection with reality from a stupor of thought, memory, desire, and frustration?

Spiritual Wakening is returning to our more complete consciousness in very clear terms. We are all part of this as we feel and feel the larger dimensions all around us.

Though we are all waking up, we are becoming more and more conscious of it these days.

This is a normal phase, as we all wake up sooner or later. Expanding times are the place we can share, help each other and learn together about the awakening process.

All shifts as we pass through this consciousness, and as if we are all turning inward! Our reality is changing what we thought was. Did you also see this? That means you become conscious of your awakening!

When our view of ourselves changes, our thoughts change every day. "It's hurting to think these days," says Geoff Hoppe, Channeler and Crimson Circle Creator. We believe that the way we do change. We are switching to our spiritual intelligence, our sensual intelligence from relational thought. We pass into our hearts and out of our brains.

This is an example of what we mean by saying it hurts to think. Let's say you go by the TV or on the radio, and there's a burst of news. Will you accept it fully as you used to? I'm not that. I'm not. It's like I'm seeing or hearing it, but it isn't the same as it was.

What about the more worldly life problems, such as to-do lists, appointments, or tracking which day of the week or what time? Have you recently missed appointments or forgotten words since your childhood? I got! I got! I had to laugh at myself the other day because I held a fork in my hand and couldn't remember the expression.

I would think that I've lost my mind or developed Alzheimer's if I did not know about The Shake and our spiritual awakening. But it's simply a Symptom of Wakening, I know, and it makes me happy. It reminds me of the incredible evolution we are undergoing. What makes it all the more unique is knowing and expressing this knowledge, as the media will have us believe, with people who experience change but do not realize that this is not a negative change.

Choose what you want and choose what is right for you. Avoid situations that are frightening or contracting to you. Remember, you are the maker of your life, so choose for yourself what resonates.

As we make this transition, we move away from separation and move towards a common consciousness.

CHAPTER 9: HOW TO ACHIEVE SPIRITUAL AWAKENING

Look at an Indian guru or a Buddhist Monk, and you'll find that their face gives them a dreamy look or a state of bliss. Because most people, particularly those living in the city, are burdened by deadlines, aspirations, and intentions, the desire to disentangle themselves from worldly concerns and insipid considerations can often be a blow. Some end up traveling, and some depend on friends' company. But after weaving pessimistic emotions, someone will most certainly find himself again in tension until he returns to the stranglehold of the real world. So after initial attempts to find solace, what's the best cure that failed? The summary can be in two words: spiritual awakening.

Spiritual awakening is an operation that takes place inside an individual. It includes increased awareness, illumination, and transcendence. How do we hit that condition exactly? Does it mean we are reclusive and concentrate as scarcely as possible in a single room? Perhaps that, however, is an advanced method to achieve spiritual awakening.

A full understanding of the functioning of our mind is essential. All the results of our mind and its procedures are around us, both visible and intangible. Human perception is restricted, and the only products are what we feel in our surroundings. For instance, take color.

Color is just the quality of the wave-length allocated to the brain.

The color itself is just a trick, and when describing a particular object, we can not say that red or blue is an absolute fact. We must take away the mind, in trying to try this exercise, in the knowledge that perceptions of the human brain limit our mind. You should watch the mind as a casual observer and regard it as something different from us. Try to relax and concentrate and make sure you are alone from external intervention.

Imagine that you are in an unseen dome, and the mind is outside where you cannot penetrate possibilities and fancies. If you do this, deep silence will come, and you'll think you're free to think about it. Faster, larger, and more inclusive, you'll sound. And you will have a look at reality instead of the false reality that our mind perceives in the state of increased consciousness. You will feel peaceful and feel more and more profoundly connected to everything.

This requires a lot of discipline and practice. And you allow yourself the opportunity to be alone and where nothing can bother you. And there is nothing. You are second nature in attaining spiritual awakening through daily training, and this enhanced awareness lasts longer. Most importantly, this practice will help you raise your living standards.

Spiritual awakening is a very individual experience — every person who goes through this experience seems to have a specific way it happens. It is also referred to as the dissolution of human consciousness and the fusion of unity with all objects. It is ultimately defined instead of a unique, one-time occurrence as a continuous journey.

How do we know if we did it? What are the indications of genuine spiritual awakening? The question arises whether we are going in the right direction as we are closer to awakening.

• Intensive power surges;

• profound upliftment and unwinding of the mind;

• extreme fear and death experience; and unexpected awareness that there is no I

• and feelings of peace and happiness previously unimaginable;

unconscious signs of spiritual awakening, and approach to them along the spiritual way;

These are all entirely subjective symptoms, and all the time or suddenly, they have been recorded to start. Knowing about it will allow us to use it as "diagnostic instruments" to explain the distinctions between insight and insanity or to seek assistance to find answers or obtain healing when necessary. This research method will reveal new and useful insights that can help create a change in consciousness.

Notwithstanding such signs, the transition is an essential player in an awakened spiritual journey. Most of us as seekers feel that our daily lives need a change. As soon as we can determine what changes are needed, the sooner we can use switchgear, the more we can move into life, another symptom of being 'now.' The more we can move into the rhythm of life. The frequency or severity of symptoms may also lead us to get out of our habits or routines and change our lives.

Spending time with spiritually based books, audio, and video – and a lot of knowledge from the internet – can help us encourage our journey in the future. Many genuine awakened teachers have videos online, and it's a very good way to adjust their state of being and incorporate spiritual practice.

There is an advanced method of meditation that can lead you to a spiritual awakening directly.

And this closes your eyes and sees what's beyond all reflection here. There is a subtle experience of life beyond thought. You can feel it. You can feel it.

This feeling will grow very quickly if you give your full attention to it. If you have the discipline to concentrate on what is beyond thinking, you will have a spiritual awakening in a very short time.

But thinking takes you out of it. What happens is thinking. So many ideas emerge to capture your attention and re-identify your thoughts. Thought emerges, and your attention as a reflection goes to that idea, and you become the thought.

The mind wants you to stay with feelings. Your focus on the mind empowers the mind and its nourishment. Then your mind controls your perception if your attention is to be thought. If you turn from thinking to what is beyond thought, consciousness is inspired, a spiritual awakening starts to occur.

To concentrate entirely on the feeling of life, any thought that comes out like a hot potato must be dropped. You ignore the thoughts with extreme focus; your mind is turned away from thinking.

This is not a method of meditation in which thought witnessing works because even that requires a certain level of thought.

Your concentration on what's beyond the mind should be so intensive that thoughts can not even come up. It takes a lot of intensity because you want to identify with your feelings. It's a strong tug.

Just when an alcoholic wishes for a beverage, one drink, and all the pain goes away. Same thing with the thought: Just let your mind return to thought, and all pain and intensity will disappear.

It can be really serious, moving entirely outside the mind because it can be painful. And in thought, there's a certain joy.

But the more you practice this meditation, the more passive it is, the more you can relax, and spiritual awakening can happen.

So it takes a lot of intensity, a great deal of attention to stay away from thinking through what is above thinking and in what is below thinking.

And saying that you don't break it off because you can't stay there. It is not anything or a place; instead, the lack of objects and locations, the absence of everything known, is eternally fresh and new.

And you know that this absence is the light of bliss through the deep practice of this meditation technique and become a light bulb of bliss.

Very soon, for a person who has the discipline, spiritual awakening will happen.

Are you thinking of meditating?

In all documented history, there is proof that humanity has always looked for its higher self. We somehow appear to know that our life exists on this planet or must exist for more than a few misty years. Today, we were past the time when religious dogma was important in humanity's consciousness if only to offer hope for a better future.

Suppose time passes, and human consciousness is increasingly conscious of the more fine energies that make our bodies what they are and all the other things that our five senses can understand. In that case, we become conscious of the finer forces themselves and understand them in at least somewhat.

So we're starting to wonder. Suppose I am not this body that I can see and feel, but it consists of atoms, molecules, etc. Something like my physical body manifests the even better energies behind the small things which give you order and intelligence. What am I? What am I? Am I a spiritual creature? If so, why don't I wake up?

Luckily for humanity, the Enlightenment came to give us the tools that can help us gain knowledge in such questions and even answer ourselves across the ages.

Many people seek spiritual awakening. According to those who have reached one stage and progressed well beyond the awakening to a higher awareness, it is a worthy ambition to have and accomplish. Many have come to this world, such as Paramahansa Yogananda, who tells us that divine union is possible and offers us the instruments we can use to achieve it in our everyday lives.

When we advance along a spiritual path, we become like a metamorphosis in awakening to finer energy.

We start changing from a higher state of existence and realization. We start to improve. Our spiritual awakening begins—our real identity as a spirit and not as the physical body is beginning to be realized. We steadily gain in our ability to understand and realize our true nature with the proper guidance of a self-realized teacher or guru and our efforts along the way.

Many people who tried and practiced good meditation techniques find that meditation gives them calm and the opportunity to deal with challenging problems in their lives regularly. You find that your higher mental energies are awakened and can use and trust your instincts more, heal yourself spiritually, and make some spiritual healing manifest in those around you.

Many understand meditation as the basis of any spiritual, psychic, and personal growth. This was determined by several experiments by modern scientists in the medical community. They also advise patients to find and use a meditation method for relaxation and stress alleviation.

Maybe one of the reasons why meditation has become a valid cure to many human ills in the general medical community is that they do not need a belief in God or a greater force... Meditation is what anyone should do to manage and mitigate a disease or unwanted condition, at least in their lives.

One thing that takes control in this way is that sometimes it leads to spiritual awakening. It accepts responsibility to heal itself. However, for most people, the outcomes seem very similar—better awareness of one's whole and happier and less fearful existence. This awakening is different.

CHAPTER 10: SPIRITUAL AWAKENING - FROM THE UNREAL TO THE REAL

"Lead me into Light from Obscurity, from Unreal to Actual, from Death to Immortality." Priest in Sanskrit

The voices of mankind are roaring in an agonizing rumbling over our world for the unreal. At this din, it raises above all a voice like that of the Golem by Lord of the Rings, "My precious....my...all mine," that echoes the voice within us, clutching to the increasingly material things.

Each of us has an illusion façade. We assume that we know our true selves inside this facade. We nevertheless attach our identity to the unreal façade.

This front joins all the false stuff around us. In a war inside us, the façade struggles as most of the world's goods represent and sustain the illusion that the façade is filled with more products, clothing, vehicles, homes, and wealth. If we were more sensitive, we would sense the discomfort created in our bodies by this distortion of reality.

We can only understand what money is available when electronic bits transfer without a true value from one device to the next. Neither has our paper money any true worth because the gold standard does not back it. We also embrace the illusion of the worth of money, in itself, as gold has no internal value.

We exist in this unreality in which we kill life. Our souls are crushed. It causes misery, suffering, and pain. However, we desperately hang on to our unreality out of a fear that all the material 'substances' that we have accrued will cause us more misery.

What if we could go outside this unreality instead of still being stuck inside? Will we be prepared to take the measures needed? What if we were able to gradually loosen the grip on us? This would mean a transition to the longing of spiritual awakening in our consciousness from material accumulation and comfort.

The desire and practice of approaches to get more light into our physical bodies are among the first stages of spiritual awakening. It means moving from the outside to the center of improvement of our internal lives. When we undergo a "soul fusion," more light reaches into our bodies. It helps to know our true self by receiving more light, moving from reality to reality, and from death to existence. Our Real Self is also known as the sacred spark and our spirit.

I listed a merge of souls that can take several years or lives. It happens as we become a complete manifestation of our soul in consciousness. Our souls influence both facets of our conflicting personalities.

Our Soul substitutes for the visions in our minds of our unreal selves. The seed of delusion closely binds us to our unreal selves. This seed loses its footprint in our body, and the only remembrance remains that finally also disappears.

However, we must go through the suffering and the pain for the seed to dissolve. There is just an illusion outside. Outside.

Lana, the healer of energy, describes her experience of the seed of delusion dissolution on her journey of spiritual awakening. She woke up and fell upon her with the weight of the delusion of all mankind. In her ears rumbled voices of all of the fake selves in the universe. In every cell of her body and back and neck, she felt the illusion of the world. She was afraid that from the pain, she would implode. Her partner, a powerful healer, held her left and right occipitals physically. He was in an empty, neutral mental place, with emotions or reactions as she writhed in agony on his floor.

Unwilling to continue with her surreal self and the perception of life, she walked through the agony that moved her body and head and into the front lugs of her brain, where she saw the light flowing through an inner vision. Then, little by little, she felt her body moving down to her tailbone and legs. The wrong, the unreal self's delusion eventually got out of her body. She felt it as a giant tentacle jellyfish.

The Moola Mantra performed the music during Lana's ordeal. Two Masters from India, Amma, and Bhagavan, were spiritually awakened. They mean, among other things, that it awakens the divine presence in our souls. It sounded like the voice of liberty for Lana and like the breath of the Divine moved her body. When the light came into the body, her body returned, opened like a rose.

Based on her different experiences, she aligned more with her life goal, which means that the human DNA is re-aligned.

I think that most people do not know how they are attached to illusion. Like the human beings of hermit crabs, the sands of delusion still turn towards consuming more and more material. Like some hermitian crabs, some people look for a bigger shell to settle in and feel better for fear of violence.

The fantasies of our unreal minds lead us to rage and assault. These delusions cling at all costs to life that keeps us stuck in pain. In reality, we strike ourselves only because we only fight against our suffering, like one arm wearing a knife and slitting off our other arm.

It only believes in the illusion of existence; our unreal self has no life. We need assistance in unlocking the belief that our physical bodies are locked. Teachers inside and outside will carry us just so far. In physical bodies, it is necessary to carry us on the rest of the way to waking spiritually awakened beings. These awakened beings represent the Divine Grace, the other 50%, through which we will be released from suffering in eternity.

Tips for Spiritual Awakening through Healing

It is not surprising that you cannot think clearly if you deal with an inconvenience - whether in the flesh or emotionally. A troubled mind means that the inner being and the escalation to enlightenment are challenging. Inevitably, without spiritual awakening, you would experience self-pity and despair.

Most people would seek spiritual significance for their earthly nature sometime in their lives. Many people have a profound urge for a holistic spiritual cure to achieve spiritual awakening. In this modern age of medicine and technology, this profound search for spiritual cure may seem odd. Many people want a life that remains straightforward and less complex. Although not wrong with me, the progress in medicine and technology is an excellent and marvelous credit to the men and women who have taken pioneering steps today.

The mind, body, and spirit are treated in spiritual medicine. The concept of "light and love" is used for good minds, bodies, and minds by non-physical healers. It relaxes the body and releases rigidity and fear. The release of these unwanted thoughts often enhances self-healing and forgiving stimulation.

Thus the fundamental belief of spiritual medicine is that, depending on your religion, you can have a connection with God or gods and at the same time obtain a healthy, good sense. Spiritual healing teaches you the inner confidence to seek support from others. Spiritual healing is about taking care of yourself and everything around you.

What are the spiritual cure methods? In various ways, it can be done. It is possible to achieve spiritual healing through prayer, advanced meditation level, healing power-sharing techniques, and individual awareness. Both types of spiritual healing help people better or slow the effect of illnesses.

Instead of blind conviction or illusion, all spiritual healing methods should be achieved with a completely balanced view of the philosophies. In the coming days, you'll receive the light by experiencing spiritual healing with complete comprehension.

Seven tips to achieve spiritual awakening by easy cure:

1. You should eat a stable diet and practice often

2. As you and other people do.

3. feel your region.

4. Don't forgo your objective/s.

5. Don't be afraid to ask for assistance.

6. Recall spending time with family and friends. Friends and family provide you with comfort and proximity to healing.

7. Make sure you always remember your intent and only the meaning of your life you can understand.

So you can reach your whole health and start your way to spiritual awakening with the aid of a spiritual healer. Through spiritual healing, you balance mind, body, and spirit and start your transition to self-healing.

How to Have an Instantaneous Spiritual Awakening

An instant spiritual awakening will take place. It is very straightforward.

Make your full attention to the following exercise. It is possible to have an instant spiritual uplift that will lead you to experience the Self beyond the experience of body and mind identity. You will feel like shapeless, conscious energy.

The first thing to understand is that through the senses, you cannot know the Self.

It is not possible to taste the self, see the Self, hear the Self, sense the self, or touch the Self.

Take this into account:

You've opened your eyes.

You see and mark what you see. You see.

"This is my body, you believe. This is my machine. That is my computer. I'm typing on the screen with my palms."

And instantly, your mind marks what you see, and you conclude that these labels are valid automatically. You look at your hands, and your hands name them. And the keyboards you type on appear very physical, strong, and separate.

But keep your eyes closed and stay quiet.

Tell me about your hands from this quiet point of view. It doesn't move or look at them. Where and what are they if you can't see them?

It would help if you told you that you feel your mouse or keyboard holding your hands. What's this sensation, however? How do you feel when you call your hands?

You must forget to define your hands, feel what is beyond the words, and have an immediate spiritual awakening. Learn what's beyond thought here in addition to the five senses.

Forget about describing your body with your eyes closed and feel what you call your body.

Not a body part but the entire thing.

There's the feeling with your eyes closed that you're here, but feeling it instead of describing it as a body, a name. Feel what's here feeling.

Feeling untouched and without words, feeling. Here, do that.

Anything you can't identify here; you can't explain it correctly.

Since there are no limitations here and the senses cannot be identified.

However, there is a living memory.

Knowledge of what exists is there.

Existing and consciousness in this regard are the same—these three things you can't distinguish. You're here, and you know you're here.

You can't absorb this or understand this. You must close your eyes and immediately let your thoughts go and feel them.

Close your eyes and notice your current experience. You will instantly experience that what you are is not solid, that you have no borders. It feels like shapeless strength.

You went beyond the mind and the body here. You had a spiritual awakening instantaneously.

And you can see that this spiritual awakening is not a coming and going condition.

This experience of being outside the mind and body is still here.

Now it is just a matter of holding your attention here and focusing on this experience of yourself outside your mind and body — the experience of formless energy.

You had an instantaneous spiritual awakening quickly if you practiced this exercise. And every time you do this simple exercise, it becomes visible, simpler, and better than mind and body. It leads to more spiritual awakenings.

CHAPTER 11: SPIRITUAL COUNSELOR FOR SPIRITUAL AWAKENING

Have you a tight relationship right now? Is it becoming more and more difficult every day? You and your life partner can need spiritual awakening. What is it doing? What is it? How is it that you submit to a spiritual awakening? Is that going to help revitalize the relationship?

It's not always a response to planning for this harsh chapter of your life in marriage, division, or division. Now both of you would take a hard and long look at what you've been doing for years.

A spiritual awakening undergoes a great deal to rebuild your old relationship, as at the first stage of married life. But couples who have a rocky relationship should first consult a psychologist or a wedding advisor before making that move. But This is an obligation to ensure that no psychotic episode occurred between them. It is also a long way for both parties to gain a deeper understanding of their relationship.

Since a counselor addresses the happy couple's emotions, it's not enough to correct the pair's problems. You have to find a spiritual, mystical, or psychic psychologist for yourself separately. A counselor will help the couple articulate their thinking and emotions. They need a spiritual healer, a psychotic, a mystical when it comes to paranormal and spiritual awakening.

The advice that these professionals bring to the pair helps determine better spiritual weaknesses of an individual, which are factors that strain their relationship. The spiritual advisor will do things to help get the person's intimate experience out of the past, even whether he/she causes the current split with his/her partner.

A spiritual advisor, mystic, or mentally is also powerful, which clarifies the unresolved issues of previous lives, divine awakening, or contact from someone else... It will help the person understand what they have encountered and help him understand and acknowledge what happened to his partner.

Understanding and acceptance mean a spiritual awakening between them, which is better because the happy couple will save the relationship instead of fully dismantling it. If the couple were faced with their spiritual defects together, this time, they would be easier to approach with greater honesty and sense.

It is important to note that you can change your environment if the glad couple wants this spiritual awakening. This is when you want a spiritual change and decide to be an enhanced human. Being a happier person means that they'll start giving more time for meditation and contemplation and less time for events in the other world.

Old Spiritual Awakening Rituals

Spiritual awakening is a goal everyone seems to like. People seem to be in search of spiritual union and enlightenment in the prehistoric era. Similar old practices are performed worldwide by various groups of people. Indigenous societies, which remain to date, show us how ancient people want a deeper understanding of the world and the spirits.

Rituals are, unfortunately, regarded as from the old world and are not recognized today. It is brushed as a primitive, superstitious, and unreasonable activity. The Church opposed these practices and called them heathen, which the Church denounced. By this, people understand and travel to spiritual awakening. Through these rits.

In ancient times, mystery schools were devoted to discovering, exploring, and touching upon the mysteries of life. In Egypt, Tibet, and Persia, the schools were flourishing.

In various locations, such as the holy lake created by humans and the underground chamber under the Great Sphinx, the ancient Egyptians toned unique chants and sound at midnight. This singing and sounds activate a portion of the brain, opening the brain to general electrical energy and stimulation. This will unlock your mental talents and abilities. This can free. Once it is opened, the individual can experience more psychic and spiritual abilities. Gifts will encompass intuition, imagination, farsightedness, and strong skills.

Besides, the end of the year in ancient Egypt is recognized as a measurement, contemplation, and spiritual enlightenment. Usher Rekhat or Mother Worship begins with a practice of meditation that increases the awareness and devotion of the followers. Meditation also attracts the ritual shares to knowledge and wellbeing.

Homa is an ancient ritual for Indian fire to help you have good ties, find your wife, have children or even eradicate bad karma in your horoscope.

Tantra is used to convey and promote spirituality in Buddhist and Hindu traditions. Tantra is not a practice but rituals that preserve a spiritual heart. Tantra means the Internet and illumination, the term itself. In ancient India, this has been used for spiritual awakening and progress. Tantra is now a sexual/psychological phenomenon. The ritual, which formerly was an awakening route, is now used for sexual perversion and spread among pornography and prostitution.

Old Iran also has a special way to see spiritual awakening and illumination. To achieve awakening, spiritual perfection and later immortality of the soul are necessary. In understanding God, too, Spiritual strength is necessary.

Interestingly enough, the production of thangka paintings in Tibet leads to establish attitudes such as harmony, patience, perseverance, focus, self-development, and spiritual lighting. Thangkas paintings are similar to the art of pasta Chitra, which was first recognized in India. The old methods continue to be used today.

Until now, most Indigenous Tribes who have started these rituals still practice and trust them until now. Suppose these rituals are authentic and applicable. Spiritual awakening can be realized by taking different rituals among different areas; the person who is seeking spiritual awakening should begin this inner and self-communications.

The Spiritual Awakening and True Happiness Process

First of all, I want to mention that for everyone, this phase is not the same. Some processes are identical but do not make any mistakes, but the essence of the experience is different. The spiritual awakening phase has always been portrayed in the history of Zen Buddhism by so-called the 10 Ox-Herding Fotos. Each of these images showed one part of the process of awakening.

Starting with the need to achieve inner harmony.

At this point, there has happened something that has caused the truth you know to be thoroughly questioned. This incident may have been traumatic, or you may have stumbled over it, or it may have even exploded as from no part of the world. At this point, finding inner peace and true happiness is still dark, but you suspect that they exist and want to find them – the end of the cry from beyond the veil to you.

Process Awakening Number Two: True happiness is coming but is not there.

At this point, you have seen the ox somewhere and somehow. Somehow there has been a moment when there has been an inner calm that defies logic, but how and why it is unknown. Nevertheless, experience is sufficient to catapult the spiritual awakening process. You know that there's an ox out, but it may not be easy to locate it again.

Patience and attentiveness.

At this stage, without much luck or, rather, hard practice, you can't go farther. This is the stage for reflection, self-exploration, and consciousness practice.

But you will struggle with your personality, and the ox will not listen to its orders. The Ox will punch her head more often. Although the beast goes free, it is beyond your reach as you orbit closer to spiritual awakening, but it gains steadily.

Mindfulness and patience.

Oh, oh, oh, oh! You've finally picked up the ox! Nevertheless, realizing true nature is not the end. Still, you can see that your journey has only begun after you have recognized your nature as an awakening, not cognitive but experiential. It becomes clear that after you are finished by loving your discovery of true happiness. Ox riding is a mastery that never finishes, and you start.

Water carries chop wood.

This is probably the most neglected aspect of the awakening phase, probably because it is the most complicated. It may well be special to you how awakening enters every dimension of your existence; the source will guide where you go now. The ox itself shall lead you at this point, but true steadfastness and inner peace shall be a lifelong growth. Part of this process is supposed to be a mystery, but you can learn it quickly enough. Good luck in your development; you did it a lot before.

CHAPTER 12: ARE YOU READY FOR A SPIRITUAL AWAKENING?

Wow, are you prepared to awaken spiritually? Will you benefit from the great spiritual awakening that takes place in our own time?

How do you tell if this spiritual awakening is ready for you?

These are the attitudes you need to know when you are ready before our very eyes for this great spiritual awakening.

The first indicator that you are ready for this spiritual awakening is your lack of fulfillment. You may be rich or poor. You may be ill or well. You may be regular or impaired, or you might be a person. You may be advanced or illiterate in academics. But if you are unhappy with how things are, then it is a sign that you are ready for a change, which this spiritual awakening provides.

The second sign is that you have tried several other things to rid your present life condition of this frustration. You didn't find someone you expected to succeed, who would certainly satisfy and last.

Perhaps you tried religion. You go to mosques, lectures in the Bible, religious associations. But in life, you remain hungry for better things.

You should have tried drugs and alcohol. They have temporarily offered you relief. But then you have become more alcoholic and more drugs, and worse than these, the brittle feeling of lack of pleasure and completeness in life.

You may have attempted sex with other partners in the hope of having the ultimate sexual excitement, to be disappointed and maybe sick from fatal venereal diseases.

You have maybe tried to live well, be disciplined in a decent life, without religion, to do good to yourself and others. But you have no good reason to be still afraid that many pleasant things in life, such as a safe body, and the comfort of a family, are missed by this sort of life.

And the third indication that you're ready for this great spiritual awakening is that you hope there's a better way to live than you have found. You didn't get desperate. You know that there is a way out of the meaninglessness of life deep inside you.

You are prepared for the great spiritual awakening when all three of these behaviors are yours.

You may ask me, does anybody have to go through all those miserable life experiences to be ready for a spiritual awakening like drugs and irresponsible sex?

Not for that. Not for that. But several of these interactions have to be passed through to understand their ineffectiveness. I had to go through hollow religious rituals to learn that there was no way out of meaninglessness in these rituals.

Major Spiritual Awakening Signs

The three principal signs of spiritual awakening are emotions that are becoming a hallmark of our daily lives more and more people experience every day. Our spiritual awakening signs embody and are a small part of humanity's spiritual awakening as a whole.

Quiet Desperation

The mass of men leads to life in silent despair, Thoreau said. He regarded spiritual awakening signs, but the cause was not addressed in this example. This is the sensation that our view of the world is wrong, that something is missing. Our full vision is a strong thing that allows us to achieve our full potential. In His image, God made us, and He is the supreme insight; He is all-seeing and all-knowing. Our complete vision must be identical if we are a representation of Him. The limiting of our understanding of our spiritual state begins to frustrate our soul. Silent despair is a reminder and a symbol of spiritual awakening for us.

Creeping Dread

It's a message from our soul or our unconsciousness. Crushing fear is one of the most popular manifestations of spiritual awakening. It tracks and stores 99% of the experience we experience, while the conscious mind can only track one percent of the other... This part of us notes every little detail that we experience in our lives. When our conduct becomes too mechanical, and we forget our goal in life - the creation of consciousness - our soul notices and makes us feel afraid to remember that our time is finite and precious. We have to look again at how we use it.

Inner Emptiness

This is the one that tells us most that we are ready for any sign of spiritual awakening. When we have thought that things we are concerned about within this universe are turning into dust, it is time for us to be concerned about everlasting things and never fading in the afterlife. This is real comprehension. It's not when awareness has advanced past our mind to the heart level that we fully internalize; when it gives us the true value in a change of behavior.

You most certainly would instinctively notice one of these symptoms of spiritual awakening. It is impossible to witness these symptoms of spiritual awakening if we are living in this secular society. You must take action if you haven't done this before. These feelings appear only to reside on the edge of the consciousness, and they're not enough to allow you to live your life without addressing them. But you can live in a half-life that is completely unlived before you get up and start looking for answers.

A mechanism that can be improved with brainwave training, a validated technology that changes your brainwaves to shift your frequency to the desired state, awaken, or lifts your consciousness spiritually.

Spiritual awakening is regarded as a sacred event through which the transcendental essence comes into contact. You acquire knowledge of the sacred, which is an undesirable state of altered consciousness through spiritual experience.

10 More Signs of Spiritual Awakening

1. Your prayer or meditation changes. 1. It sounds different when you try to pray or meditate. Thousands of ideas rush to the front and confuse your intent. You have difficulty concentrating. Give this knowledge to this cascade. It could be that Spirit injects emotions, tells you that He knows what you are praying or meditating on, and the rush of messages is quicker.

2. Hot flashes are experienced. It's an energy rush that you experience. It just takes one minute to heat or refrigerate. It could be so intense that it makes you nauseous for a moment. Go through flow, and a sense of connection with God replaces this feeling. Heat may come from your hands, particularly when you are around someone that you feel is hurting.

3. You know you've got a lot of flu. Dullness of the head, back, neck, stomach issues, muscle or cramps, pulse, chest pain, libido changes, and addiction or pain in your limbs may become part of your daily routine. Your body purifies, as is the area of your aura. Have a doctor look at the illnesses and, if no physical signs of disease exist, be aware that it is just a temporary symptom of spiritual awakening.

4. You feel a deep willingness to free your life from something restricting. You can find like you have to change what you do or want to be around for a living. Perhaps you want to say "find yourself" on your artistic side. Go with the flow. Go with the flow.

5. True and lively dreams. You can begin to dream lucidly - a dream you are controlling. You may also be "visited" by the deceased or by your spirit guides. Don't let you be confused by the dreams. Since they are real, they sound real.

6. You seem to have gone back in time. 6. When you clear your emotional problems and release past

convictions, you become literally "lighter." You have a higher vibration. More optimistically, you see life differently. More light fills you up.

7. Events can change your life drastically. Divorce, death, home changes, sickness, job losses, and other disasters will occur at this time. Your world extracts all of your attachments to the physical when you wake up to your spiritual side.

8. You get drawn inside. You can lose interest in what is happening globally and concentrate more on the meaning of your own life.

9. You didn't even realize that you could have surface capabilities. The world is all about imagination, which begins to develop in you. You are very imaginative and can reveal an ability that you have never before shared.

10. Illusion. You want to make the operation quicker. At the end of the proverbial tunnel, you can almost see the sun. Brainwave coaching will speed up the process.

Spiritual awakening positively transforms you and your life. However, to wake, you must purify your mind and deal with feelings and events that you haven't dealt with.

CHAPTER 13: WAYS TO EXPERIENCE A SPIRITUAL AWAKENING WITHIN YOU

When I say most people sleep spiritually, I mean they don't use their spiritual skills or strength. They are like people living but not going around the house, not doing anything because they are still lying in bed and still dreaming. They are like people. Here are three ways of living a spiritual awakening to awaken your mind and perform the spiritual works.

Notice all about you and your link

This is a bit of very easy advice, but many of us do not. It's not even half the material stuff around us that we go through life, much less the spiritual things. We don't see the diverse forms of the trees around us, the majestic arrangement of the clouds above us, the small animals on the ground, and a thousand other objects before us. If we don't understand the things we can see, how can we know the spiritual things we cannot see?

When you begin to realize the objects around you and their interrelation, your consciousness will be unveiled with a world of superabundance, a world full of the infinite procession of life. You will find the smallest bacteria that spoil your food and know that the two classes of creatures interrelate with each other.

Unfortunately, this partnership cannot be found for a reason. What is the relationship between bacteria and the sun? They are much too distant to be closely related. So we're right. But if we start to see relations in what we see, we will surely discover the connection between objects that are far farther away from stars that our human eyes can see.

We know that plants are associated with the soil in which they grow. Toss them off the ground, and they're dying. Fish are also connected to the water in which they swim. Take the fish out of the water, and they will die sooner or later. We know that people are connected with this world. Take people without support structures off the planet, and they are dying. The connection between these items is evident. But when we understand that these items are connected to material objects and objects with meanings, we find that any entity has to do with any other object, specifically because both have significance.

Bacteria are linked to the stars since they are both meaningful entities. Bacteria are used to purify our air and to convert matter into fertilizer. Regardless of how far away the stars provide the heat the bacteria need to live and multiply.

When we understand that all things are linked, we start looking at the spiritual aspect since that connectivity is invisible even to our physical eyes. The spirit can sense it only in us.

When we perceive these links of all things, we wake up from our spiritual slumber and undergo spiritual awakening.

Consider your relationship with the people who have gone through this Earth.

Your grandparents went away, but once on this earth, they were here. In some cemeteries, their bodies are laid to rest, but their souls are here yet. This sense of presence has probably not been maintained by anyone except by the Chinese. You are looking at the image of those who left this planet earth through death and seemed alive and capable of communicating ideas with you. Why is this? Why is this? It's because you still have their souls. In the things they have created, whether it be a chair, a book, or something else, their spirits live.

You connect with them when you begin to sense their spires' presence in the stuff they left you. They will always interact with you, and you would be shocked. You may not have to attend a meeting with those who have been on the way to communicate with the spirits. Talk in your heart with them. He used to call regular conferences with dead people, such as George Washington, Napoleon Bonaparte, and others, the renowned Napoleon Hill. At first, he was scared to show the public that he took part with the spirits of the deceased in these conferences. Subsequently, he believed that this was not an uncommon behavior and should share its advantages with others.

Suppose you have a healthy association with the spirits of those who have gone away one day. In that case, you will wake up spiritually realizing that you are surrounded by many minds who are keen to connect with you.

Pray Always

Most people do not observe the two terms. You pray when you're in trouble or need something you think you can't accomplish. They forget that through their influence, they can do nothing.

You were taught a number of prayers when you were a child, but you believe that your prayers have outgrown. You believe you're mature and you're yourselves. There can be no further reality. You have to pray more, not only for more things but more often as you get older. And even in the most stressful activities, you must still learn how to pray.

I once found out about a group of men who pray in monasteries rather than priests or religion. They deal with electric cables. They are liner. The priests or the men and women religious go to their mass and prayers. But they normally spend their time in their jobs after that. But the linemen must pray for electrical wires to be installed or repaired. When hanging on the poles, they continue to pray for sudden death. You know that with a small mistake, you may lose your lives. They continue to pray for being protected from electrocution after their service, with thanksgiving. These linemen tell me to pray 24 hours a day because they don't know when to fix an electric line. Unable to foresee emergencies.

You will be on the path to a full spiritual awakening within you if you will still pray and talk to the Soul of all Souls for all matters to you.

There are three ways for you to witness a spiritual awakening:

1) Notice the whole thing around you and its connections;

2) meditate about your connections with the people who have gone through this earth;

1) Notice the whole thing around you and its connections;

The word spiritual awakening is quite much used and perhaps for some very obvious reasons is misunderstood. Through the 12-step movement and, in particular, the 12 stages of Alcoholics Anonymous, the word itself became very popular, as the twelfth stretch says: "These steps gave me a spiritual awakening.

In trying to figure out what the word is, it may be considered in the twelve steps, as it offers a sense of peace and clarity that is likely to help clarify. In the initial twelve steps, there was some discussion about using the word "spiritual awakening" or "spiritual experience."

At last, we choose to use the word spiritual awakening. While AA literature does not provide any particular explanation, part of the reasoning was that an awakening indicated a continuous phase. On the other hand, experience suggested a kind of one-off case - even though none of them is valid, this implies the two concepts. In healing, much focus is put on alcohol recovery or some other way of life. People like the notion of awakening in this way.

Trying to describe the meaning of a spiritual awakening is a far harder task, and only someone who has had one can paradoxically really understand it. The lead to the twelfth step in AA lists several steps or steps a person takes to change his or her main dynamic within him or herself and his or her world. But you come to identify it, and it is the core of it – the inner clock is wound back and begins with a much healthier and happier spirit.

Have a Real Spiritual Awakening

To have a spiritual awakening, you must surrender.

So we want to get you out of the key notion of being an educated and intelligent person and into what is here beyond these ideas at this moment.

The subconscious still tries to get it right. But when your subconscious gets it right, you're out of sync with what's here.

Unconsciously, the spirit has a picture of how an ideal person is, and the mind continues to do so. You're not conscious; you're not deliberately. But when you do so, you cannot be touched by spiritual awakening. Life cannot touch you. Life cannot touch you.

Therefore, it is to be mindful of the first step of surrender. Know how the mind wants to place all in a clear pile of understanding and justifications.

The second step in giving up is to let yourself go. Allow yourself at this moment to be bare and crude. Experience total sincerity right now without any suggestions about what it might be.

The secret to spiritual awakening is this truthful consciousness.

We call ourselves someone in time, someone with previous experiences and memories. But I want you to go beyond the concept of thinking and to experience what is here.

And it's just here now, and then it's gone. In this realization alone, there is such equality.

Only this moment will you feel. You can't and must sense it in mind. Beyond emotion, beyond the intellect.

Come on full with what's here. Take to yourself and fall apart and experience what remains in this moment.

Then you'll always feel peace. You will get an awakening spiritual. You will realize the silence under it all, that silence which only reveals itself completely when you come.

Without a truly enlightened teacher, this isn't easy to do. If you sit with a truly enlightened instructor, you will obtain the actual energy of Shaktipat, which awakens you in your very soul. This makes a hundred times simpler the process of spiritual awakening.

CHAPTER 14: SYMPTOMS OF A SPIRITUAL AWAKENING

Soon, thoughts and views, preconceptions, and abstractions are obscuring the bright eye of the infant. The ego's burdensome armor is embedded with a simple and free being. It is only after years that an impulse comes to retreat from a critical sense of mystery. In this moment of beauty and strange pain, the sun springs through the pines, and the heart is permeated like a paradise memory. We become seekers after that day. Matthiessen Peter

A few of us are not looking for. What makes us human is the desire to search. But few know where to look, and far fewer try to understand that our hunger is a spiritual hunger... a hunger to awaken to the mystery in which we once understood hunger. Our soul knows that it is a hunger to return to this location.

The tale of the golden bowl is the metaphor that best explains my spiritual journey. That's how the story goes. One day a soul came into being and was put in a gold cup. This soul's light was radiant and shining. People from all parts came to see the incredible light from the golden bowl.

People started putting rocks in the bowl over time. The rocks have been called socialization and behavior. Some of the rocks have been termed terror. Other ego.

Other ego. Some of the rocks were nickel-creative...conditions that distorted reality. Finally, until a day, the light became dimmer and dimmer, and not all the rock placed into the bowl could be seen through. The space became black.

In a world of separate things, the soul felt this was a separate entity. The maps from the past used to be meaningful, but the soul didn't know. They had not known that by its distortions, ego, fears, wishes, hopes, convictions, and certainties, they looked at the universe. He didn't realize what he saw was just an illusion — the shimmering shadows of real life.

The mind, however, was a natural search engine and tried to fill emptiness and hunger with the things that seemed to arise from the prestige and the performance. The more hungry she tried to feed, the more lonely she became, sad and depressed.

One day, sitting alone on the coast, the waves on the sandy beach breaking, something changed. It was an insight flicker that lasted just a moment, but wisdom reached the mind. ...suddenly, it knew the outside world's thirst would never fill. It started to look inward from that moment on.

The soul learned to look at the truth on the edges of its ego as the years passed. She knew that her ego was still there, but she did not give the soul's identity anymore. The soul knew it was not just ego.

They learned to be careful of the energy they were sent to the planet. It was less offensive and sought to avoid harming other people.... physical or mental. It became more empathic, more compassionate, and willing to practice mutuality.

He has come to see the world around him profoundly. When they spoke, they learned to listen profoundly to others. It accepted a vacuity of the ego and on both sides of each issue started to seek the facts.

It was not conscious again that it was a bright light in the universe. She did not know the whispers of those around her who wondered how illuminated it was. He used his talents so much to do as he was born. In the universe, it was changing what it could only do.

The signs of an awakened spiritual being.... the illumination of a spiritually awakened soul is manifested.

The Path to Spiritual Awakening

It appears that the aim of each one is how to attain spiritual illumination today. Different primal rituals by various people are carried out all over the paleolithic era. Humanity seems to be on the mission of a godly unity and arousal. Native people still alive today show us a preliminary view of how the world and the spirits had a deeper sense of our ancestors.

In different places such as the holy human brook and the secret compartment under the Grand Sphinx, the ancient Egyptians harmonized distinct voices and resonances during the witching hour. The vocals and sounds supposedly stimulate a head section that opens up the brain to global energy and electricity. It should release or release your spiritual gifts and skills. When unlocked, the person who has moved you - intuition, imagination, clairvoyance, etc. - will undergo the psychic and spiritual awakenings.

Ancient Egypt understood how the spiritual enlightenment would be counted, thoughtful, and moved at the end of the year. Ushet Rekhat - Mother Worship was one of her practices. This practice started with a ritual of reflection that strengthened the disciple's knowledge and devotion. The ritual of contemplation will also attract people who share understanding and wellbeing.

An old ritual of Indian fire called Homa is performed to help you get a wife, have children and eradicate bad karma or dangerous facets in a horoscope. Tantra is used to guide and cultivate spirituality in Indian and buddhist practices. Web and enlightenment are the words Tantra. Tantra was used for spiritual illumination in Ancient India.

Thangkas from Tibet are intended hypothetically to cultivate attitudes such as serenity, tolerance, commitment, attentiveness, self-development, and spiritual illumination. The thangkas are similar to the old Indian patachitra craft. However credible, these ancient practices are and apply now, are still practiced and believed in most native tribes that began them.

These old practices were a way of achieving their spiritual goals for our ancestors. Anything you choose to get spiritual awakening is an unforgettable and enlightening journey, and there are several practices you can choose from among Yoga, meditation, budgetism, etc. Find your spiritual journey with fun.

It is said that nothing can be done to bring on the spiritual awakening - the grace is given it. However, it is proposed that we should prepare the land for it by making it available for ourselves. I understand what it means to survive happily in the current instant with as much awareness as possible.

Therefore, the fastest way for spiritual awakening is to use several different meditation techniques daily, which can help us become conscious. And this knowledge can be brought to all aspects of our lives.

I have learned time and time again from many spiritual masters that lighting can't be done by doing - it's the ultimate stop that enables the quantum change of consciousness to take place. However, for most of us, all we can do seems to have to be done before we get to the stage that we can give up. Giving up at such a low level that giving up occurs, and we, our identity, cause ourselves to disappear into universal awareness.

I've tried some methods to help me live more at the moment with a relaxed consciousness that inherently gives life more fun and joy. Osho's Dynamic Meditation, a combination of physical action and catharsis accompanied by silence and celebration, is the most intense and effective technique that I've found myself.

Osho made the comparison that the best way to pull them out is to rest a hyperactive infant so that they can sit still naturally. Our contemporary minds seem to have to "lay it bare" until they can quickly become meditative.

I have had the luxury to take part in many retreats and retreats, which were beautiful. But they have become more of a vacation in the world for me. It's best to have a routine practice that is part of my usual lifestyle to bring a meditative awareness into my everyday life.

I have seen an Adyashanti quote in which many believe that illumination is a changed state of consciousness. He says that lighting is the ultimate condition of living in unchanged life—it is our egos modify reality based on all the lenses through which the world is seen. Therefore, possessing an ego gives us a changed state of awareness, and a lot of energy takes us to sustain this sense of changed reality.

Illumination is a relaxation of the way that life is experienced.

Try to wake up spiritually.

Many people are looking for something to do when they discover a non-dual message. Since the mind gets no answers, it's looking to do something to address what it believes is desired. Over the years that I sought and sought fulfillment, I always looked for what I felt needed to do. I've been looking for a method, a course or a stage, a journey I can calculate. I thought that action and initiative produced results, and they did, of course, comparatively. If a house is built or a car is fixed, at least.

Long-term emptiness

I found, however, that any results on the 'spiritual road' I managed to produce quickly vanished or disappeared completely. I might imagine for a brief time that I had, for instance, achieved a condition of presence or silence. I can feel deep thanks or appreciation sometimes. All these so-called "results" have come and gone. They were transitory, transitory countries. Everything came and went, like their opposites, bliss, ecstasy, bliss, harmony, quiet, calmness, presence, consciousness.

What seemed to push me in my quest has been a nagging feeling that something was lacking almost always. My most frequent emotion was desire and longing. Therefore, I spent years wondering what I wanted. Why did you have this desire? My life, emosic well-being, work, and relationships would be analyzed, and I would always search for something to satisfy my constant companion's sense of want.

There was something wrong with me to feel this way, I wholeheartedly believed. I wouldn't have been so vacant and unhappy if I had been more of a success. Anything I felt MUST be lacking. And as the years went by, I was increasingly looking for what was lacking.

I still had to change what I felt was lacking. But typically, I figured I could do, have or be something. I spent much time 'working on myself, in the futile hope that if I had a happier, more meaningful, spiritual existence, I would be forever feeling of lack and loss.

Occasionally I would find and follow with resolve and enthusiasm what I felt was the missing piece of the puzzle. I would always 'get' the missing piece of the puzzle, only because it wasn't the missing piece, after all. A void still existed. My puzzle is not yet done, not yet finished. With the need, the desire, and the feeling of being incomplete, the feeling of disappointment will return.

The Explosion of Oneness

The illusion of separation started to crumble when I saw that the sense of lack, emptiness, and longing was a symptom of the belief and experience of separation. Some people looked inside and never found this separate from me. All I found was what was going on, space experiences, awareness. In this, what was happening appeared to be mindful of the experiences that had occurred and vanish.

Since then, a series of explosions have been appearing, each shaking the foundations of this distinct sense of self. The explosions are not caused by any technique but seem to be triggered by the initial perception of a separation illusion. These explosions occur without any effort, without any practice or measures. The plain understanding is all that happens in these blasts. It is more precise to state that it 'bees that' unexpectedly, and in this case, it is seen. But no one can see separately.

There is no gap between what you look at and what you see. There is no division, and the two are one. This whole universe, you and I included, emerges and falls as one. Looking from a time point of view, it seems like an organic phase. One explosion after another, the foundations being shaken, the individual sense of an individual self is more and more collapsing or weaning, as Tony Parsons says.

Less Doing and More Being

Well, yeah, it can sound like a phase. But nobody does. But nobody does. And it is seen that nothing at all happens when it is looked at. The concept of emancipation is another idea, a description that sounds like something else. There is the only release. In it occurs the tale of an illusion phase that wakes, weans back into existence. This story is also here.

It's something we want to do to get us. As awakening occurs, spiritual awakening is painfully clear that I cannot do. In awakening, there is very little to do. You may assume that when you are, the awakening itself happens, which often happens for everyone. We would search for some road to get there when we assume that there is somewhere to go. This is not it, and we exist in the delusion. It's that.

You will still look for something to do before seeing that you want to do everything you do. No magic place is to be reached. The lane, the road, is the place to go. The leadership. In each move you take, the magic is in progress. There is no endpoint and no finishing point... each step towards, each step away, each phase constantly comes. You can't get there. You can't quite finish arriving.

Signs of Spiritual Awakening

This is, for anything else, a moment of spiritual awakening. The status quo is no longer satisfactory for so many people.

It doesn't do what used to work. There are far too many people worldwide who are knowingly linked in the same way to Spirit, Source, and Angels.

It is less and less tolerable to walk or to go in a "fog of forgetfulness" to what does not happen around us. We know "something else" is there than we were led to believe and embrace physically as part of this Earthly Journey.

12 Spiritual Awakening signs are present here:

1 - In your heart core a burning desire to know what your goal is

2 - you want to make a difference

3 - feel your skin doesn't suit too small in one size.

4 - friends begin to drift away from you because you no longer have the same 5 - searching for answers to questions about metaphysics.

7 - about making changes to how you felt and to think about your life

8 - to stop being content with what things are, or what they seem to be going

9 - to break the cycle of feast or hunger (prosperity, relationships, customer attraction, self-handling)

10 - to tap in and trust yo...

11 - "Something More," you know.

12 – It is unnecessary to face the fear of the unknown because to remain "where you are."

In a world that feeds fear and uncertainty, turmoil and confusion, it is no simple journey. It is spiritual.

To be willing, even when it feels or seems as if everything is falling apart around you, stepping above everything you've ever know takes bravery, power, and determination.

It is not a faint-hearted spiritual path and the desired "why I am" kind of guy. This is such a tough affirmation, and the reality is therein.

A spiritual awakening is a path, a journey of life with many layers, stages, and revelations...... self-reflecting and learning.... letting people, places, and things go that no longer align or resonates with you...

When you start to awaken spiritually, your life is never the same. More peace and harmony can be experienced.

You doubt values, and you let go of negative beliefs and substitute them with positive ones that sustain you, your hopes, and your objectives.

And more open your heart and mind to the infinite possibilities and your endless, untapped potential are attracted to you by like-minded people and opportunities.

CHAPTER 15: SATISFYING THE SPIRITUAL AWAKENING

Spiritual awakening is achieved by seeing the environment in which people exist so much better than some understand it. In this respect, it increases your awareness and becomes more and more aware of how things are around you. This is why people must understand why their spirit must be awakened and not swamped by materialistic and mundane longings. If the spirit is awoken, you will satisfy yourself and the world around you.

Learn to see a different light from the world

You are also learning to see this universe in a whole new light as your mind is slowly awoken. The world we once saw as a place filled with capitalism and materialism suddenly becomes a new place in which we feel happier and happier. Also, you can see how your mind transforms to the real light when you open it. You can turn it into what we want once you know it. Without a doubt, you can make it work and allow your mind to understand how our environment works to attract more good things.

The growth of spirit means the transformation of attitudes.

So you must also change your behaviors to grow your spirit. The world we saw as a place filled with bad stuff could transform into another place filled with positive energy. Also, you can see other people in such a different light when you understand our world this way. Then you will understand that while you cannot know everyone who lives on Earth, we can do something that will change their lives and behavior. So, from what you have learned, you should learn positive things. You should make sure what you do is produce good results. They should be nice not just for us, but for all of us.

Sharing and teaching spiritual development

Finally, you should also find goodwill and teach them what you have understood to live a spiritual awakening. Others need to learn more about your recognition to increase positivism everywhere. With such a strong interior spirit, you can easily build better connections with others.

If you need a holistic approach focused on the above-described things to evolve your spiritual awakening from inside. Moreover, once you have grasped all of it, it will all be too simple for you to deal with and avoid unpleasant things in the universe.

You should start with an active meditation technique to have a spiritual awakening. You perform an active meditation technique with effort.

Here is a basic meditation technique: repeat the words "I am" quietly with every breath. On inhalation, repeat "I" and on exhalation "am."

Rely on the fact you are there when you do this. Not like a name or a person. However, I feel like you are present right now. Feel it as a feeling, undefined, described, or judged.

Using this method of meditation, "I am," the mind will be concentrated, and the spiritual awakening will take place in such a way that you are conscious of yourself. You will realize the 'self' as your self-experience as consciousness itself, as being itself outside the mind and body. You feel healthy, weightless, shapeless, and happy from mind and body.

Once this meditation technique is practiced to the point that you can become conscious, it is best to transition to a passive meditation technique.

A passive meditation technique helps it all to be as it now is and knows it is a feeling.

Let thoughts come and go without being trapped in it, let the body be as it is, and know that you live right now. Allow yourself to experience completely the sensations which arise right now.

No effort should be made with this technology. You should be concentrated, but at this moment, you have to rest and allow yourself to be present with what is and allow everything to be as it is.

You will begin to feel like something is happening on your own with this passive strategy. You can see ideas that arise and vanish, the body that exists, and even meditation itself. You are meditated simply by allowing your experience to be as it is and to watch. This recognition is a great spiritual awakening in itself.

Through Near-Death Experiences

Survivors of near-death encounters inevitably often share stories of out-of-body experiences. This fantastic experience gives them a spiritual sensation of awakening. Why does the experience outside of the body still turn the receiver spiritually? Can the knowledge beyond the body enable us to attain enlightenment?

Many would observe that spiritual illumination is connected with saints, yogis, and lamas. When an average person encounters spiritual awakening, it can be both exciting and awesome. Some people go through meditation, yoga, and so on purposefully to lighting. Others have a spiritual awakening before their death.

The author of 'On Death and Dying' said Dr. Elisabeth Kubler-Ross, "And then you can begin to see that your lives here are almost nothing but the full range of choices you have made during all the moments of your lives when you first see what life is all about here. Your thoughts are just as true as your actions. Your thoughts are responsible. Every word and action affects your life and has affected thousands of lives, and you will begin to realize."

Some results from almost-death-related encounters are: viewing the doctors and nurses who work in your work, walking through a tunnel towards the light, gaining information. The survivor can feel that he is at peace inside. The spirit part of the body and encounters other beings, including family, friends, and so on. The survivor is unable to return to the world of the living, one of the common features of this almost-death encounter.

Below are some of the psychological changes that people undergo after almost a death:

1. Many soul members, regardless of their earlier convictions, begin to believe in reincarnation. Perhaps since the soul is separated from the body, they realize that the body is nothing but a cover for the soul or the spirit.

2. LOVE - many survivors who become generous and caring.

3. Psychological — many survivors develop extra-sensory awareness as they return to the living world.

Many who go through the above psychology adjustments after a near-death experience may be counted as spiritual awakening because they are transformed into new individuals.

CHAPTER 16: BENEFITS OF SPIRITUAL AWAKENING

Apart from realizing yourself, there are other advantages you will gain from experiencing a spiritual awakening. The awakening of personality and the self-transformation contribute to a properly adapted life. Lastly, the same healthy life leads you to a happy and happy life. You must understand what spiritual awakening can do, for you are far more than mere physical advantages. You may not know it now, but when you finely enter the condition of spiritual illumination, you're glad you've been through the whole experience.

It would be best if you had meditation to understand spiritual growth. Meditation has a lot of advantages. In this busy environment we live in, it can release ideal tension. Living and working in the city may affect the mind, body, and spirit. Daily meditation can help to release healthy life stress. Meditation can lead them to discover their true selves and form their real potentials.

You should be aware that meditation effects can not be immediately felt. You may feel a little tension from your meditation; however, you will gradually experience the effects. Remember, a certain degree of peace and harmony will take a while to feel; however, it will come. You will start feeling happy about yourself and your surroundings, for example. Perhaps you'll find the best out of a situation and not always feel unhappy or annoyed. Perhaps it would be easier to go and can join more people. You might notice, however, that your consciousness is best understood. You will maybe find that your physical body is growing; healthy; your emotional and spiritual status is interconnected and equal.

Keep in mind that various meditation techniques are available. In reality, there are various schools for the discovery of your true personality, offering diverse styles and methodologies. Many will demand that they have a motto (a word that you have to repeat to quiet your psyche to instigate the meditation procedure.) Many can find it the best way to achieve a peaceful mind that someone guides them through the meditation process. It should be recalled that the ultimate goal in meditation is to reach a safe position where you are fully relaxed and can get nothing, including your mind. This is an awareness stage where you have no wasteful thinking; play a role. Take in a black space for yourself. You see nothing; you know that you are a living being. You see nothing. It's like you plan to do in a practice of meditation. Look at yourself and realize who you are without thinking. A higher consciousness level is what

The way someone feels or sees things say a lot about him. Others can't look the way you look at things. We all have different approaches to various aspects of life.

We can all consent, however, to one supreme reality: our spirituality or spiritual awakening. It is important to note that religion and spirituality are different because they allow you to choose the paths you want to follow.

Ever since the importance of spirituality in their lives has been recognized, and continual attempts have been made to awaken and reinforce their meanings...

What are the stages and the spiritual light?

An individual who doesn't have a spiritual sense may not know the meaning of life. In short, we have to contact our spiritual side to realize the true nature of our strong life. Spiritual lighting is a state which makes you see beyond the vision of your eyes. It allows you to believe in God's power and helps you understand the basis of creation, and to feel open to more certain life truths. We may continue to live our lives, believing that strength, fame, and money are significant, but this is not true. Worldly stuff can't please us for long. Happiness from external sources cannot be achieved; it is rooted in yourself. You have to look within yourself, and spiritual awakening allows you to do this.

There are three stages of spiritual awakening or different degrees of spiritual awakening:

The first stage will enable you in your environment to feel comfortable and calm. You are living in the moment without thinking about what you could or did in the future.

You will relate to the world around you in the second level. You feel synchronized with the setting. You will find joy in life's most insignificant stuff and believe you are one with nature.

The third and final phase of enlightenment leads you to believe that you are not associated or synchronous with everything around you or that you are "everything."

What are spiritual enhancement benefits?

Some of the many advantages of spiritual growth:

- the sense of unity or unity with everyone.
- Increased self-esteem and awareness.
- To live a life of more importance.
- Feeling quieter and more peaceful.
- Purity feelings.
- Greater people's empathy and compassion.
- Better bond spiritual.
- No negative sentiments, bed.
- Improved mental skills.

How to attain spiritual illumination

The state of spiritual illumination is in different ways attainable. Here are some of these ways:

1. Let your ego go

If you think healthily about ego, you may know that it's just a manifestation of our thoughts. Often ego can ruin relationships and make life very bitter. Let this adverse emotion go and accept positive and humble positivity. You must understand that emotions of this kind can scare you and even your living relationships.

2. Stay honest with Yourself

It is vital to be truthful with others, but to be real is one of the most important concepts of spiritual illumination. It might not seem simple initially, but it can quickly come to you when you are on a spiritual journey.

3. Let Go of Your Fears

Often because of our doubts, we are afraid to do something. Instead of making them feel low, you need to take on your fears. Spiritually illuminated people do not allow their worries to influence them and do whatever they are told to do.

4. Learn to Forgive

You may feel hurt if your goals are not met, and you may take them to account for your despair. However, it can hurt you more than anyone else not to forgive people or resent others. Make peace, forgive others and also forget yourself.

5. Detach from Worldly Things

Wonderfully, it could give you temporary happiness. But the earlier you calm down, the more you get nearer to spiritual liberation because these things cannot give you happiness. However, to separate from worldly things does not mean to live a life of solidarity, but to be unreliant on material things for happiness.

6. Meditate

People attempted meditation for the longest time to reach spiritual illumination. Meditation is a perfect way to move from the world to a mental stage where you can become self-conscious.

7. Yoga

Yoga is another way of achieving illumination. Yoga allows you not only to feel safe but also to achieve calmness of mind and peace. Daily yoga practice allows you to turn off your inner voice and to think from the outside.

8. Pilgrimages and Praying

No, in this case, we do not confuse faith and spirituality, for we know that the views of each vary completely. But faith will also allow you to achieve spirituality. Since you transport yourself in a physical meditative state when you pray or visit religious sites, which can help you communicate with your inner selves and soul and achieve spirituality.

9. Learn to Love

Love is one of the strongest feelings in the universe, and many spiritual leaders believe that nothing can be achieved in this world without the strength of true love. You must love your soul, love your neighbor, love your surrounding world. Life gives rise to deep feelings of peace and relaxation, which contribute to your spiritual illumination.

How do you know when you are spiritually awakened?

You may ask if you know yourself are on the right track until you start making all the changes in your life to reach the highest level of self-awareness. Ok, here are some spiritual awakening signs that may let you realize that you're doing the right things:

- You may be less interested in the future, and the past as the present becomes more important to you.
- You can childishly see the world, and your outlook can shift towards life.
- You will be more in line with your thinking and feelings.

- The spiritual power that rules the world can be more mindful of you.
- You may be at peace; internal tensions, fears, and concerns may not exist, but only calm and peace.
- You may attach greater significance to compassion and feel more compassionate towards others.
- You do not feel disconnected from the universe any longer, but you do know that you are a part of this totality or unity.
- You may not be afraid of death anymore when you know it isn't the end of death.
- You could be surrounded by nothing other than positivity that can help you feel good.
- You may have a broader outlook, and trivial issues may not bother you more; instead, it all becomes trivial except spirituality.
- You may not want to restrict yourself any longer to the world's identification when you realize that your life is much greater than just your name, caste, or belief.
- You can feel happy and even appreciate everything you have.
- A greater sense of morality and friendliness to others can envelop you.

- You can find comfort in nothingness; you can find peace, calmness, or silence by doing nothing.
- You do not feel drawn any longer to live's material pleasures.

Are you looking for answers to questions? Now we are debating some questions about spiritual awakening, which are often asked in this section:

1. When do you get Spiritual Awakening?

When you are linked or more in harmony with your soul and mind, a spiritual awakening occurs normally. You have a true sense of harmony, satisfaction, happiness, love, and independence when you make the connection. Often it can be not easy to get here, but once you do, you realize the true meaning of your life.

2. What triggers the process of spiritual illumination?

In their lives, people will achieve spiritual enlightenment. Some may occur gradually, and some may reach the stage due to dramatic life changes such as certain major diseases, medium-life crises, divorce, a loved one's death, tragedies, etc. In plain language, your life experiences will cause the enlightenment process.

3. A Slow Process is Spiritual Awakening?

Whether or not this is a slow process is difficult to tell, as some can reach this stage quickly, while it can be a life-long battle for others. You can even hop in and out. You may be in the peak stage of awakening at certain times, but you may be struggling with self-conflict or anxiety on other occasions. It's all-natural because we are all human beings, and it's normal that we twist and make mistakes. This misunderstanding or distraction takes place because we often fight to stay on the road. We're drifting away, after all. That is all right, but the real war goes on and looks for the facts again.

4. Will Spiritual Awakening Begin with a Disaster?

Yes, misfortunes can often also start your spiritual journey of awakening. You begin to visualize life from a completely different viewpoint as you deal with tough circumstances in life. You are often forced to the endurance limits, which ensures that the mind enters a point from which it can begin to look at things completely differently. Thus the spiritual awakening process will begin.

Sometimes you wonder about the unpredictability and ambiguity of a spiritual awakening that there are no clear paths to achieve this state of mind. But the fact is that our mind has infinite possibilities, much like the vast endless universe. When you make attempts to release it. You might not even know what is inside it. In this piece, we have explored some efficient ways to attain spiritual awakening; we want to use those tips to find the true direction of happiness and self-awareness.

CHAPTER 17: HOW TO UNLOCK YOUR FULL BRAIN CAPACITY

Nothing recognizes as it will seem, but life can be very fun if we break our boundaries... so we live.

A) human being,

b) spirit who enjoys the feeling of being human. There are three sides. But we have split from the spirit because of nonsense. Now we are reconnecting and

c) the heart core of divine Light that is your bond with spirit and universal understanding, e.g., LOVE...

Frankly, spiritual awakenings do not exist unless you essentially awaken the human side to understand the spirit is still present. You're never spiritual, and you're spiritual; you're still spiritual. Anyway, you are spirit, so there's just you.

As for the full capability of your mind, this is an element of being awake with the spirit; hence, your main and only concern is to know your full capability through the spirit. Don't get stuck in hyper-nonsense, but rather embrace the infinite possibilities that you can grow with spirit. You can also learn that what you think as a human being is something other than full brainpower.

However, optimum psychological wellbeing is essential as Maslow has taught us how to love and observe awakening. Maslow believes that self-refreshed people will encounter multiple peak experiences every day while others less regularly.

If you reflect on the results of Maslow, you are very convenient to distinguish between bull ology and spontaneous creativity. Moreover, you will not be too tainted by the conventions of society and therefore be free to explore and become a spirit that is awakened, enlightened.

a) Meditate and never stop listening even when working because meditation is going to grow in motion.

b) To build one's spiritual connection with all the added benefits, previous experiences and teachings must be eradicated. It would be best if you threw away all your attachments and then some of them. Your experience is in line with spirit, not the human hand, with the awareness of relevance.

c) To appreciate alternative perspectives that shed light on our infinite possibilities, you must be as blank as a page and as clearly as a sparkling glass pane. Then you know what was previously unknown with fresh eyes, the eyes of the awakened senses.

d) Read as many illuminating books by famous writers as Wallace B Wattles, James Allen, Alan Watts, Adyashanti, and St. Germain, Shakespeare, etc., to help your journey. Naturally, the scriptures with an open mind are driven by discernment and imagination. Remember that every scripture is written symbolically, not literally.

e) In Manly P. Hall's Sacred Texts 'THE SECRET TEACHINGS OF ALL AGES,' one extraordinary piece of work is found. This is one of the brightest books to be studied if you want a broader understanding of centuries-long machinations and motives which are brainwashed by irresponsible religions and politicians, and industry.

f) A book that I just discovered, surprisingly, is also worth to be read by Guido Mina di Sospiro, a two-thousand years-old YEW named "The Story of Yew." This book has imaginative philosophies, but it tells us how society has forgotten the image of nature at our peril.

g) The utter need to discuss our attitudes to our world is what we learn when we awaken. If our path is not self-centered, we will evolve with the whole image of nature exponentially. It is highly advantageous to work with trees and other plants because we are fundamentally natural, divisive, and unified in mass and often spend time in all areas of nature.

h) to know and embrace unity as such, but to unity is a humble step towards a fully-fledged spiritual awakening. h)

We do not open the doors which have prevented our communion with universal knowledge by ourselves but by our full capacity. We thus merge with DIVIN INTELLIGENCE and seem to have woken up our brains, but in fact, they have become one with Divine or Universal LOVE. Love is all, and love is universal intelligence; let us, therefore, know love. LOVE is all.

Namaste! Namaste! Can wisdom lead you in this amazing enlightening experience?

The awakening isn't a shopping ride or a minute's drive into a religious home - it's opening your website and the first page that shows that you don't know the truth. You are born to be the conqueror, and you dedicate yourself to living in a veil of confusion, embraces, smiles, affection, and appreciation.

The look and wonder of children

Several teachers seem to agree on some signs of spiritual awakening. One is a recovered knowledge of the miracle of creation.

A Mystery To Be Lived

When there is a sense of separation, life becomes playful again. This game is well known to us and is a childhood game. The world suddenly becomes visible through wide-open, unjudicial, non-analytical, and unconceptual eyes. In a manner, the marvel of creation is rediscovered, a comeback to the unknowing. Even when we know what the universe, the senses, and the sensations are or play the game conceptually, the mystery remains.

Finally, this is all: a mystery to live through.

We are united with awe and wonder without just a logical understanding or vision of the universe. Once more does the miracle of a flor that flourishes or of rain or a lover laughing. There are only miracles, and they can be seen. The extraordinary in the ordinary is something that gives our lives a feeling of daily joy. With a sort of childish wonder, even a feeling of sorrow or boredom is visible.

Be As Little Children

What often seems to fail to recognize unity is the desire to avoid or argue with present experience. We're not insisting any longer on the fact that it is different. Free of association with the individual self, reality can be seen in all forms and still be regarded as a complete mystery. In reality, while we have words to explain it, we don't know what this is.

When we look at emotions such as sorrow, rage, remorse, or dissatisfaction, we find them as mysterious as the hidden depths of the universe. The feeling is humbling because we are completely amazed at the miracle of daily life. We are like little children (as Jesus suggested) living with no findings on the mystery of life now.

I have spent a lot of time completely captivated by everyday objects and experiences in my own life. Only breathing in and out, when fully embraced and experienced, can prove fascinating. This awesome and wonderfulness stems partly from the first moment that life is seen and experienced. We are newcomers, rediscovering both the world around us and the world inside us.

The Delight of the Ordinary

I recently headed for a coastal town in the south of England in the Portsmouth area near where I live and was amazed by the beauty of the ships lit up in the ferry port like Christmas trees. I saw this sight a lot, but that night I saw it as if it was filled for the first time with a sense of wonder and pleasure. I laughed loudly at the ecstasy I felt as I looked at it.

It is always difficult to explain the reality and beauty of the world around us. But those who report a spiritual awakening share this sense of childlike wonder.

CHAPTER 18: SPIRITUAL AWAKENING: DISSOLVING THE EGO AND SUPER-EGO

All is energy at its most basic level. This includes people, ideas, colors, rocks, plants, space, light... everything. The universe has been dubbed by many as a "vibrational universe."

Where are you beginning and ending, and where are you starting and ending? There is no energy limit. Our perception is energy concentrations with single patterns of vibration. This makes stuff look strong and distinct.

Spiritual awakening goes beyond the "obvious" essence of separation and accepts all that is harmony. Spiritual awakening has little to do in theological terms with the "finding of God." The achievement of one's energetic efficiency can also be considered.

Shrinking and Growing Exercise

It also starts with a simple "Shrining and Growing Workout" exercise.

Imagine yourself in a country house, seeing sunshine in the afternoon, listening to the bird's sing. You've got a beautiful view of the region. Imagine the personal and far-reaching views. Take all the information in your head. Look at the space among the trees. Smell each flowers' smelling fragrance. See every cloud floating across the sky.

Get it smaller now — the picture you are reduced to bee size. The house was suddenly gigantic. It's all Nice. Rosebuds' delicate are far larger than you. The cat is a huge beast, and as an object of its attention, you feel discomfortable. There are far wider spaces between objects. The trip from the front porch to the street is an incredible journey without wings. Please take the details. Think of a teacup - a little swimming pool now...

You are even more shrinking. You're a dust mite size now. The world has changed entirely. You no longer have a sense of your home. It's far too massive for you in a lifetime to try. Your world is this place. There's a couch in this space. But as a sofa, you no longer see it. It looks as big as a mountain, a massive rocky monolith. The polishing fibers are far bigger than the most significant redwood trees. You can walk through these fibers as easily as you walk in your garden between the trees. The world outside – the space – can't be seen from the fiber forest. You can now drive in stuff that looked solid to you.

They're an atom now. Your house has long gone because it's so vast—your view. You are so tiny that you are deep inside your couch with one single cotton fiber. Your world is now one single fiber. Interestingly, between you and other atoms, there is still space...

You're currently a subatomic particle. You float easily in a vacuum, finding small levels of other subatomic particles. It's still... space between you. What are these things? What are these things? It is no longer "air" because you are small outside of the air compound molecules. What about the material that comprises the air, cotton fibers, the sofa, the home... your neighborhood, your earth, your solar system, your world...

And, beyond what science has so far found, you go smaller. You are now energetic. Pure energy. - Pure energy. You are an aware, smart, imaginative force. All of you are, and all of you are. You are the maker and the builder.

Then you begin to develop. Soon your human size is back. It's been fun but let's get bigger! You're tall now like the forest. Your house looks like playback for a child. The cat is a small insect's size. You still grow... You still grow...

You're the planet's size now... and larger. Like a small blue-green gem, you keep the Earth in your hand's palm. Where is the house? Where is your house? Where's it all? It's okay, but because it's so thin, you can't see it. As far as you can see, there is no room between everything. It looks like a marble on Earth.

You're larger than the galaxy. You continue to develop. Thousands of galaxies that seem so far apart now are clustered in a necklace like pearls... what would the stuff look like if you continue to grow? When they get closer and closer together, soon, the distance between objects appears to vanish – all because your perspective has shifted.

You witness a spiritual awakening when you can understand the enormity of it. It truly is beyond our intellect to understand this fully because the intellect relies on physical sense knowledge. That little - or that big - our senses can't look at.

So is the spiritual awakening. Whatever your convictions, it is best to use the imagination and reach beyond what we perceive to find this awakening. Try it today and sense the unity of it all. Get the unity awoken.

A becoming consciously aware of the world around it recognizes that its spiritual awakening is essential and continuing. It is not found outside but within. This phase is found. The way it's? The mechanism is the dissolution and re-balancing of the ego and the super-ego. The mechanism is always changing because the ego and the superego are "persons" of the lesser will, not the godly will.

Ego Home & Super-Ego Home

Everyone knows the body is its temple. The soul plus is housed in this temple with its radiant energy signature in abundance. It's in the aura field and chakras for those who don't know the energy each person carries. Yes, that's right. These sources of energy are still being investigated, measured, and studied by science. In the lower three chakras of the body, the temple is situated between the ego's home and the superego.

The ego and superego are very high, so the three lower chakras don't surprise it. "It's my own," and "what if...," and everything else... mind chattering, the ego, and the super-ego keeps each person "better than me." The chatting of minds is known as the inner voice of what you think. It is a tilt on the radar of a spiritual awakening, whether you or anyone else says something else.

When the ego and the super-ego are uncovered during the spiritual awakening, it requires several practice persistence levels. It's not only possible for many to think that you rise above an abusive relationship and awareness of poverty and the "I can't" syndrome. Keep in mind that the ego and the superego is a camel that wants to/can/does cover up the just-right vs. the wrong.

The spiritual awakening inside is filled with self-detection, re-discovery, and remembrance of the Divine will. As the process starts, many find it easier to talk, or their reality, friends shift, and the journey has just started. Let the joy and enjoyment of the truth that you add to spiritual awakening.

Spiritual awakening is generally when a person perceives the world as something other than how others undoubtedly perceive it. In a sense, when a person develops his inner consciousness and becomes more conscious of the meaning of the things around him. This is why the need for a revived spirit must be understood to be greater than earthly and worldly desires. An individual may genuinely feel fulfilled with an awakened mind, not only with himself but with the world around him in daily life.

A World In A Different Light

When our minds slowly wake up, we will see the world in a very different way. The planet we regard as an evil place where materialism and capitalism unexpectedly become something more beautiful and conservable. Furthermore, when our spirit is opened to the true light around the planet, we can know how it turns and as we know it, we can make it grow to the points we wish for it. We cannot simply grasp how the universe works but can use it to attract countless positive points from our spirits.

Attitudes Change

Therefore, it means that our behaviors often shift as we reach spiritual development. The environment we once regarded as a negative habitat will become something full of positive energy. Furthermore, we begin to see other people differently, as we see the world as such. Then we understand that while every person living on the planet might not be known, anything we do will change their lives and the way they work forever. Therefore, we have to watch our past experiences as a way to have a far good world. We must ensure that all our efforts are directed towards a successful outcome. They mustn't be nice alone for us, but, obviously, for the benefit of everyone. Through doing so, we are modest enough to be real social stewards.

Teach other people

Another vital thing is for people to have the will to share and teach others what they've learned through spiritual awakening. Others need to understand more about positive results, so that everywhere in the area can be changed and multiplied. You can easily improve ties with other people by having a positive spirit inside.

The bottom line is that you first need a holistic approach to a life focused on the things described if you genuinely wish to cultivate your spiritual awakening. And once you've already taken advantage of each moment, it will certainly become too straightforward to go ahead and save you from the world's pessimist pursuit.

CHAPTER 19: SPIRITUAL AWAKENING - THE BEGINNING

Spiritual awakening is the mechanism by which we release our fake toxic egos and let our true selves live. By making who He made us be, we glorify God. The starting point is that we have an awareness change. There must be a sudden or incremental awareness that our behaviors and thinking are not founded on the soul (our true self) (ego-oriented). We come to know at some point that we're disappointed, unsettled, and "not ourselves." Or maybe we feel "next to ourselves." This feeling sometimes gives a sudden realization that two entities can regulate our consciousness.

Or maybe we feel "next to ourselves." Often, there is a sudden realization of this sensation that two forces strive to dominate our consciousness. This is when we can know that we are under the ego's control (the unhealthy ego). We recognize that a break from our thinking processes has to take place. We must distinguish ourselves from the mind. The aim is not to get rid of thought but to bring it back in its right place concerning the soul. A mind is a great tool to use, but we can also let our decisions take over.

A realization that a division between mind and soul needs to occur is often called ego consciousness. This doesn't mean that we stop using our thoughts, start to use them properly. Being mindful of what happens when we are affected by the ego is one of the greatest steps in taming it. We can see and sound with a little practice when the unstable ego enters. What are the signs of her approach in the future? Either of these may be signs of the danger to our true selves, the self linked to God:

o Fear

o Worry

o Anger

o Guilt

o Shame

o Prejudice

o Bias

o Lust

o Greed

o Confusion

o Envy

o Hatred

o Gossip

o Anxiousness

o Irritation

o Restlessness

Any activity that reduces the existence of a dystrophy ego is possibly a clear signal to us, other persons, animals, nature, or property. Because our dysfunctional ego doesn't belong to our true selves, we will benefit from it by acknowledging that we are separated. We will start to drift away from it by watching, right now, what we experience, how we behave, and how we respond to other individuals or circumstances. Let ask ourselves questions such as:

- "Why did I say that?" to begin creating this separation from our ego?
- "Right now, what do I feel about that?"
- "How can I explain my experience?"

These questions and the like help us get separated from our toxic egos. Our true ones might not have behaved poorly, but we behaved in a way that protects our ego against threats and helps develop, grow, and prosper while we are under a spell and control of the ego.

We start separating ourselves from the feeling or action (the 'observer') to break free. When we first practice this method, we do not forget to ask ourselves these reflectional questions until later. We probably would start by taking time to reflect on the day's events at the end of the day. This will help us improve the ability to observe our sensations and reactions. It's a safe way to do so with journaling.

Maybe during the day, something happened to make you feel sick or upset. Anyways of thinking about the incident are possible. The first starts with the sentence written in your newspaper, "I've been upset since I said it to myself." This method reveals that your rage - the ego and you are one - is known to you. An assault by others on your dysfunctional ego is annoying.

Another way holds our ego's spools in better shape, enabling God's strength to start to flow back into our true selves. We started by saying in this approach, "I was angry because I said it to myself, so-and-so. Now we have put the anger in front of us, where it can be more carefully examined. We will soon find that our dysfunctional ego, not our true selves, was wounded by this event. Once we know that, the rage disappears because what it is is revealed. The light of reality cannot be opposed. The words fired on us from another person's ego (remember that their true self would never say that!) cannot hurt our true self. We know that the event was an exchange of the ego with the ego, which protected the other person by reducing the ego. The people were not even interested in the true self.

There is, therefore, a slight but crucial difference:

- "I feel anger;" versus "I am angry."
- "I feel frustrated;" versus "I am frustrated."
- "I feel fear;" versus "I am afraid."

Ego consciousness is separating us from our ego. This gives us more understanding for ourselves and the other individual who may ignore the influence of his or her dysfunctional ego. Incidents of the day that disturb us can allow us to learn more and develop a spiritual life. These events are no longer attacks, and they are donations! You will teach our dysfunctional ego and ourselves more, now on the road to dissolution. Don't resist or give up; watch them. The process of restoring our soul and our relationship with God begins.

As you do this technique, you will slowly get closer and closer to each moment and build ego consciousness. You will not have to wait until the end of the day to know that your emotions come from a damaged ego and not from your true selves. Finally, before you have a chance to act, you catch the egg.

We seldom have to act as quickly as we think we need to in life except in emergencies. Typically there is time to think before we respond. In certain cases, however, cultural conditions also require an immediate response. A pause to consider and create a suitable answer is usually poorly seen and seen as a sign of sluggishness or weak intellect, or unpreparation in a fast-moving society. "Time is money," "If you snooze, you lose," and other slogans do not remind us to waste any time, or even a moment, or to lose ground. But it's a short-term mind, invented by egos, which sometimes leads us to great difficulties. In reality, the good at "thinking on his feet" is more time to go before us than the "quick thinking person," and in the long run, we are doing well. The time needed to process and make sound decisions causes fewer errors, strengthens relationships and improves life quality in general. In many respects, pause pays off! It's not the soul that hurried. In competition is the ego.

We only understand the difference between reality and illusion through knowledge and not only thought. Illusions, not the true self, are part of our ego. The light of consciousness, the light of reality, will decrease illusions. Once we have room between our true self and our delusions, we will react to the situation properly.

CHAPTER 20: MEDITATION AND YOUR SPIRITUAL AWAKENING

The individual sits in a circle surrounded by candles, and saying mantras or chumming is also seen as an oriental ritual. Meditation. Meditation and its advantages are currently accepted worldwide. In every culture, it's not exactly what we had in mind. Apart from the soothing effect, meditation is also called a route to awaken the spirit and begin the journey to spiritual awakening.

There are various schools of meditation. Every school will have its meditation thinking. It can also be categorized according to your concentration and various meditation methods. Meditative approaches concentrate on a field or an insight, while others focus on a single object.

Therapy is used to stimulate the mind and body. Simple strategies can alleviate tension, stress, and anxiety. Apart from the inner peace brought through by meditation, it can also enhance the body's overall health. It's also a perfect way to improve your focus. Studies show the connection of athletic and sports professionals between meditation and other concentrations.

Health benefits of meditation include improved circulation, deeper relaxation, increased heart disease resistance, regularization of blood pressure, reduced anxiety symptoms and muscle pain, allergy relief, arthritis, and major aid in surgery and recovery.

You can listen to the inner self and distantly from the demands of everyday life through this concentration process. Understanding the inner selves leads to our higher self's understanding. This will enhance our perception and awareness of how the higher unites with world. You get the opportunity in meditation to tap into your inner self and get in touch with how your life looks. Touching the inner self will help us to be happy and fulfilled.

In some religions, meditation is used to achieve illumination. As explained, each religion adapts various ways of thinking and focusing. However, the form or methodology used is not so important to meditation as the underlying principle.

Meditation is about listening to the inner self; it has to do with regulating and concentrating attention. It is very difficult for others to concentrate on what is necessary and emphasize a fixed item since there are so many distractions. If a fixed entity or area is oriented, one point may be experienced, and a different state could occur. However, this one argument is not easy to reach, and some people will need to meditate for years.

The person will experience happiness when one point is reached. Bliss is a soul's natural condition, which cannot easily be experienced in everyday life. Spirituality and the mind are expanding their comprehension of nature and the world in this meditative state. The materialistic and rapidly progressing world will spill out destructive thoughts and actions by concentrated more on your spirituality.

A more profound perception is perceived, and the body is in one with the world. This would link us to the Supreme Being, they claim. In certain ways, it may be likened to a spiritual awakening, in which the body and the mind can truly comprehend what cannot be seen or touched in the natural world.

Most people regard mediation as an East Practice, in which people sit in a lotus circle singing or humming mantras. In addition to the calming effect, meditation also means that it is a path to inspire life and begin the transition to spiritual awakening.

There are several meditation schools. Each school has its meditation thinking. Meditation may also be classified based on its focus and has various techniques. Some strategies concentrate on a widow or a background observation, while others highlight a particular topic.

One of the advantages of meditation is to keep the mind still and relax the body. Simple meditation can relieve tact, tension, and discomfort. In addition to the internal harmony of meditation, it may also contribute to improving the health of the body. Meditation also improves attention immensely.

Meditation health benefits are improved blood circulation, a deeper degree of relaxation, increased acceptance of workouts among cardiac patients, normalized blood pressure, decreased anxiety attacks and muscle pain, allergy relief, and more...

Meditation enables you to hear the inner self and to distinguish between the demands of daily life. Acceptance of the inner self leads to our higher self (our spiritual self). This understanding will improve our understanding and knowledge of how the higher ourselves unites with the universe. You have the opportunity to tap into your inner self and see your life as it sees it through meditation. Looking into the inner self will direct your overall enjoyment and realization.

It is important to note that meditation is about listening to yourself so that your focus and concentration are guided. Too many distractions will emphasize what is important and focus on stationary objects difficult for others. If you focus on a static object or area, you can feel a one-points and change it.

You will feel ecstasy if one point is reached. Ecstasy is a natural soul state that cannot be reached in our daily lives alone. Spirituality and consciousness enhance their perception of nature and the universe in this reflecting environment. The unsuspecting, rustic world will flush negative thoughts and action away by directed more towards your spirituality.

There will be a deeper understanding and wisdom, and the body will be one with the world. That is the bond between the Supreme Existence and us. In a way, it may be compared to a spiritual awakening as both the body and the mind can fully grasp something in the real world that cannot be seen or reached.

CHAPTER 21: SIGNS INDICATING A SPIRITUAL AWAKENING

We live when people have to accept their spiritual side more and more as a matter of course. And people who do not usually use the spirituality word are open to such ideas as discovering the meaning of their life and trusting their instincts.

Although we live in a world of reverence for science, logic, and reason, many people question our way of life. Even if they try hard to stop it, they are niggled by the question, "We need more to life than that?"

More and more people are spiritually awakening and desiring more in the material world than they are. "The Secret" DVD's reluctant success demonstrates that the world is willing to accept universal legislation and is left to want more.

The subtle natural, subtle energy shifts are Spiritual emergence or ascension that elevate Votre vibration to huge physical impacts. It's also a personal journey that varies from person to person, but I hope you will learn from my experience. There are ten symptoms of my spiritually awakened upward symptoms:

1. A rollercoaster emotional

You may be touched more frequently than normal and on the edge of tears. It is normal to cry at the end of a hat over the news or show a feeling you haven't wept over before. You may also be more violent or upset towards people. You feel sad some days and full of joy other days. You feel the whole spectrum of emotions, really, and yes, they are exhausting, but for some reason. Keep the emotions present, sense them, and move through.

2. Stronger connection to nature

Previously you may have "taken it or left" your attitude to nature. Ok, with all of nature, colors, and shapes, you have a profound love. The seasons begin to be welcomed, though winter was scary. You may like animals that you have never liked before. To entertain my friends who knew I couldn't stand them before, I developed a cat lover. You change and consider things more for what they are.

3. Changes in energy levels

You bounce off the walls one day, and you can't even get out of bed another day! You must roll as much as you can for this one. Down days sleep, relax or chill and flow in the high days of energy. Try eating healthily and try to avoid tension or shame, stabilizing it.

4. A sense that something about you has changed

You may feel different, but you know something has changed internally. You may not look different. Your old ways collapse on the side of the road, and the truth that you start emerging.

5. Sudden understanding of repeated trends or relationships

For decades you may have lived in the same old habits, but you get conscious of it all of a time. You can always kill what you make, choose unavailable partners or attract dependent people – the list is endless. It's great; the first step in its eradication is to become aware.

6. Allergies and cravings, and intolerances to food

As you become more energy-sensitive, your body will begin to respond to foods you have always eaten and begin to long for something else. There may not be lifelong intolerances and allergies, so remove them from your food for a few months and try again later. Your body will need cravings, so go with them and trust your body to express what it wants.

7. The need to "find yourself" and improve your social circle, comportment, jobs, etc.

Your material requirements were fulfilled, and more is to be desired. You might begin to wonder who you are and see that your current existence is more of a by-product, maybe not a deliberate decision. You could find your way out of the layers to reconnect with you, the spiritual one, before you can consciously pick.

8. An increase in occurrences of coincidence

Better known as synchronicity, helpful individuals and circumstances appear just what you need. You will be revealed with signs and messages responses to questions. Synchronicity is a warning that you are on the right path to understand these miracles. The more notice and heed you are, the more you appreciate the advice that you get.

9. Quicker manifestations

Spiritual awakening increases the vibrations; this entails the unblocking of abundance to flow to you— being aligned with a higher frequency leads to faster and better manifestations to be obtained by you. Know your feelings so that you get what or better you want.

10. A change in what you read

You're changing for the better. You're going to more complete and purposeful life. Like you, you'll find some ways to spend time and not like the stuff you've always done. It's all right, and you're interested in the latest pastimes.

Change and development occur; resistance increases the discomfort you feel. Know that all is just as it should be, and you have a human development experience; leave it alone. Ask where or what you resist, and let it go if pain strikes. They say it's just before dawn, the darkest night, so you know it's for good.

While none of these conditions can be confused with severe medical conditions, here are some more signs that you see spiritual awakening:

Creating, detoxifying, and streamlining the living

- Desire for Independence, depression and lack of interest — Change of relationships, jobs, food habits, sleep patterns, vision and perception, and libido
- Tiredness, headaches, altitude in the heart, hot flashes, and earrings
- Increasing the knowledge of your emotions (your and yourself) and more emotional answers
- synchronism, intuition, and psychic gifts (energetic sensitivities)
- Wonderful body, mind, or emotional healing

This list is not full at all, but these are often recorded signs of spiritual development.

Attacks of fear or panic.

As things shift in the body, emotions and vice versa are influenced. Many people fear unwanted changes and may resist the Spirit's effort to rid themselves of habits of fear-based thought. This can be fear, nervousness, or panic.

Anxiety is an indication that you resist the process of clearing. Accept this healing feeling. Recognize it. This broken part of your soul asks for the purest vibration of your soul to be merged and matched with. Respiring and bringing it into the life anxiety flow is just another source of energy. Remember that it is just energy going through when you feel anxious. Say something like: "I allow dense/dark energy while enjoying my peaceful, prosperous, easy life to be transmuted and integrated into love/light energy."

Use the instruments that you found and repeat mantras, prayers, and statements. By the time you memorize them, your reaction mechanism will be shifted, and you will start tackling fear newly.

By tapping on the Sacred Heart Centre, panic attacks can be "talked down." Reading a passage on a Miracles Course makes my mind relaxed and relatively easily into a better perspective. Some herbs were found to be effective for nervousness treatments. Discuss the Valerian root, passionflower, kava kava, John's wort, or some other herbal supplements with a medicinal herbalist.

Often the strong energy that you experience is an accumulation of faster frequencies to be released. The best way to do this is to spend five minutes in the

Sacred Heart. Breathe deeply, and then imagine a ray of light from your heart for someone you believe wants a boost of love and light for the God-Goddess. Send the beam into humanity's collective consciousness if you don't think about a single individual.

Feelings of the body

The old cellular structure dissolves as the biological body moves to the light body, creating a new crystalline structure. This can be an unpleasant experience for some sensitive people before enough shape is transmuted to allow a pure vibration to hold. Detoxification may result in ailment and pain (flu-like symptoms) or fatigue, which cannot be explained or treated by our current physicians. In your body or chakras, it is not rare to have unusual sensations. Pressure will be on the head, or the scalp, or the front (particularly between the eyebrows), or energy may arise in the body. There are also reports of pain, hot flashes, and chills.

Body pain and aches can be specifically connected to blocked or trapped regions of the subtle bodies. Headaches may signify the opening of the third eye. Stomachaches may mean your feelings/emotions are being stuffed. The blocked 5th chakra may be shown by chronic coughing and sore throat. These symptoms should subside until the energy is cleaned up and the new vibration acclimatized in the body. Before then, you can use energy therapy, acupuncture, aromatherapy, exercise, herbs, homeopathic medications, minerals, vitamin supplements, salt baths, massage, etc...

As the organ or glasses inside the body adjust to fit the body of the light, when you meditate or breathe consciously, your arms, hands, feet, or legs can tingle. I have felt that someone has slightly touched or played with my hair for more than ten years. I felt like I was half of my body or my mind was too big to fit inside my skin.

Be mindful of your feelings if you have ascension symptoms, as what we believe creates our reality. Our bodies are a mirror that shows us our values in our consciousness or our unconsciousness. Be sure to think about yourself and your body and say only good things; we are more rapidly than ever.

CHAPTER 22: OUR SPIRITUAL AWAKENING IS DIFFERENT

Everyone's story is different when it comes to changes in consciousness. This is because when the change starts, everybody's life is different. Some people, some individually, are married. Some people have jobs, and others don't. Some of them have a soul mate; others searched.

Some are financially plentiful, and some are emotionally tight. Some have been practicing spiritually like meditation for years, and others are new to this world.

As part of her spiritual journey, a friend of mine had cancer. Others suffer severe injuries. Some have addressed a loved one's passing. I had a big family crisis shake my boat. I had a family crisis. In many communities, indigo children have powerful energy for improvement.

Everything that we meet reflects us. We don't sometimes understand what's going on. For instance, every night, when I entered my bed, I experienced a very strong energy current. It was bright, vibrant, not bad, unknown energy. It took more than a year. Then she stopped abruptly. My knowledge was that my pulse was changing to accommodate the changing energies.

Some meet people who make them realize what's going on, and others feel that they are all alone in the dark with these changes.

And then some alms have a spontaneous satori or illumination that is happy, happy, and elevating. And even so, the strong messages demanding change will create uncertainty in their lives.

The ego challenges all these situations. And it's pointless to resist.

What's up with all this? In the Middle East, what's going on? What's the whole story behind all these changes in weather, climate changes, volcanoes, earthquakes, and tsunamis? The planet has evolved. We are changing our culture. We are improving ourselves.

We assume the planet earth was, metaphysically, not too long ago on the road to destruction. We wrapped things up and came to the end of the Mayan and other times.

We passed a worldwide coordinated meditation in August 1987. The Harmonic Convergence was named. This occurrence has an extraordinary relationship between planets in our solar system, the Maya calendar, and astrological rituals from Europe and Asia. The dates also differ in that the Sun, Moon, and six of our eight planets correspond to the Grand trin. That's what happened physically on earth.

It was even more important what took place in the heavens. Planet Earth's inhabitants choose to opt for us not to allow the survival on our planet to stop. We have chosen a new path for our world. Our world has changed location in the solar system since that date. There have moved the magnetic poles. Slow but gradually moves towards Russia, the northern magnetic pole of the earth. Florida's Tampa International Airport has already forced its runways to reflect the movement of the magnetic fields on Earth.

Furthermore, the ice caps of the planet melt at record rates. The waters of our seas, rivers, and lakes will then be refreshed, and the stocks of fish will grow, and the numerous terrestrial livestock population will increase. Also, new species can evolve, and the discovery of ancient species that we thought were gone far from the ground.

Landmasses change more rapidly than in documented history through tectonic plates, volcanoes, and fluvial change.

We are recording new research findings, including embedded microprocessors for our bodies, new power sources, and particles that seem to be moving more rapidly than light speed. Physics Today is proof that the Buddha spoke of things centuries ago. Research by scientists, such as the experiments by Tesla, has long been thought pointless, proved to us to be accurate and useful.

Why does this all take place? People develop. People evolve. We wandered in the nebula of dreams for too long. We have lived lives separated and separated from the Source, God, and Universal Energy – whatever you call it. We now find that the bond that resides in each one of us is very powerful. A link to each other and a link to the spiritual world from which we came. We name this spiritual awakening, illumination, transition, etc. There are only marks by human beings on spiritual events. Regardless of the mark, the interactions are real and massive cohesion exists between many worldwide—a kind of one-minded experience of major transformations.

We can't tolerate dictatorships or tyrants. We no longer permit others to take care of our money, happiness, or freedoms, like teachers, religious officers, governments, financial bodies, prophets, and others. We find ourselves educated, our own lives managed. We're free of the bonds, and we all get in our way. We're no longer "following the king." Our internal voice is followed by one of us.

This you may have felt recently in your own life—a feeling that somehow you are unconnected. You're no longer healthy. You've been uncomfortable with people and situations before. You feel that objects, old theories, common principles cannot be grasped. You quickly lose concentration. Within your mind, you hear more self-speaking, leading in new ways. Inside your skin, you feel awkward. All these are physical signs, and many of us happen simultaneously! It's changing our physical bodies, minds, and climate. We are bound more than ever in documented human history to the metaphysical side of ourselves. Don't combat these shifts because they won't be good for you. Ask your God or your Angels or your divine powers for guidance, or whatever you believe. Please ask your eyes and mind to open. Seek, you're going to find. Ask, and you will receive it.

Spiritual Awakening Through Illness

Let's take a realistic look at it: Take the instance of repeating influenza attacks. How do spiritual awakening gain and opportunity come from grip?

1. Priority: You only do what is needed or necessary to cancel appointments, calling on work to let them know that you are not well when your body becomes exhausted by headache and fever. You don't waste time or think about insignificant, irrelevant issues.

2. Focus on Health: You become more health conscious, mindful of what you eat, drink, and what outside influences you expose yourself to.

3. Speaking the Truth: You might be telling people to stop talking when you're physically, mentally, or emotionally not able to take in more. How often does it happen that you keep your mouth shut when you are well because you want to be 'nice'? When you are sick, you are more honest with yourself and others.

4. Looking after Self: When you are feeling low, you have to take your own needs seriously—looking after your body becomes a matter of self-preservation.

5. Less Ego Fixation: If your illness seriously weakens you, you will no longer be bothered making a point. It becomes less important to 'be right' and more important to 'be well.'

6. Sticking with the Essential: When you have throat pain, for example, you are only saying what is necessary, leaving out all the fluff. Similarly, you are less attached to being right or being heard and trust that things will sort themselves out to the previous point.

7. Allowing Help: This is a wonderful opportunity for people who find it difficult under normal situations to accept assistance. You must learn to embrace and welcome support when you are sick and can't do some

things. It is also a lot more enjoyable to support you, the person that helps you so you won't hear: 'Oh no, I can't, I can!'

Must you get sick to learn or do that when you are good?

There is a lot about spiritual welfare, but is it central in the life of a person? Why are divine beings discussed? Is it essential in ourselves? Does it have other good features? To respond, we must first consider the value of spiritual well-being. It is a sense of an individual's physical state in entirety and of your being only one of its kind. As stated quite clearly. All of it concerns our inner lives and how they contribute to the outside world.

For many people, the journey down the spiritual path can belong. It's all about where we begin and from what we look at when we begin the healing journey. The impression that you are only one such thing may be a better way to understand the value of a spiritual being.

The question is whether spiritual growth has any benefit; we can tell that; there are many. First, you feel happier about life. You will feel your life's fulfillment and the value of truth. The stuff in your life can be balanced and managed. Better connections can be established. You will feel meaning in life and even mental well-being because you are more influential in your emotions. Thoughts that quiet your mind to awaken your spirit.

Spiritual development also enables you to experience a strong bond to a power larger than yourself. Therefore it's confused with confidence too much. To undergo spiritual growth, you don't have to be religious.

What would you do for moral good?

- Spend a while meditating and dreaming about your life about the positive. This will lead you to understand the positive stuff behind the spiritual path.
- It is also of great benefit to enjoy nature.
- Begin working on the development of constructive and toxic partnerships.
- Admit that you differ and cannot change people from you.
- Recognize
- Talk to someone who has experienced spiritual growth. It will help you to show where you can find answers.

There are only those aspects that allow you to achieve spiritual well-being. It's got a lot more. Extraordinarily, be more aware of the things you are to do and the things you are to do and concentrate on spiritually developing to be healed and pleased.

Spiritual Awakening of Society

What was the defining idea that moved the wheels for the spiritual development path of society in which we are currently involved?

The period in my view, was in the early 1960s when a significant section of society wanted to step away from conventional thought and behavior. As the word spread, the numbers grew quickly and the 'sixties,' when love, drugs, rock, and roll came into being.

Anyone present in this timeframe can note that it was a dramatic and rapid change in the participants' thought processes. The momentum was never stopped.

What brought this whole moment in history to be defined?

The spark that kindled all of this was the idea that "There must be more for life." That is the short version of it, and to better grasp all the sense behind it, one must look deeper into the thinking patterns of society.

It is easy to see that the word "more," which means everything from adventure to money, gives us little insight. This is why it is important to examine the way of thinking of society. In the early 1960s, most people got up in the morning and went to work to get enough money to purchase the materials they thought they needed.

You felt that you don't have to be remembered as the "more" contributing individual in society. I grant that you don't want to start your spiritual developmental journey with free Love and Drugs. It's a way of beginning things, but it was a start that brought about a wake-up call in society and made the mind think.

Society acted like a child who lives in a home with very strict rules in place. As soon as the child is released, he or she will let down his or her hair and try to taste the forbidden fruit, but in due course, he or she will get the new path and calm down. It doesn't matter when you take a look at society's attitudes in the 1960s.

Since the first break-out of society, they became conscious that the "more" they were trying for was not in freedom but in discovering and improving capacities to give them the essence of the "more." This new pattern of thought has been strengthened by the understanding that there were coincidences when necessary, much of the time, to guide us in the directions

This gave more power to the "more" by reflecting on whether these coincidences are occurring as needed, what, or who controls them. In turn, this led to the idea of how much power we can pick or build if anyone controls us. This, in its turn, raised the question of how to practice the art or talent if we have or will manipulate these coincidences for our gain.

The snowball began rolling down the hill and gained momentum, as did the spiritual development movement.

As you can see, one should not evaluate the social path or just the face value of an individual. For the sake of growth, it's always more helpful when you figure out what drives the move and find the silver line from any situation we face.

You see, the growth is less rapid than a negative attitude. Suppose you can't think of any other explanation. In that situation, the driving force must benefit your personal growth, or you will blind your eyes and remain in the herd that will not take the first step in making and developing decisions.

You are the one that controls your future, not your people. Do not be threatened by anyone to pursue the direction of spiritual growth.

CHAPTER 23: ACHIEVING SPIRITUAL AWAKENING

The 9-mile path crossed Florida's rare Torreya pine landscape with steep pines that followed a crest along the river Apalachicola. The physical challenge of reaching the end of the trail was overcome with high humidity – the body's total energy was invested, and no reserves were available. The traveler went through the cool stream as she bathed her worn-down feet.

The tree orders you over 200 years of age, always astonished when a first encounter takes place. The extremities hit the floor like columns supporting the expanded canopy. Lying beneath the tree on the field, your glance has been drawn upwards, and you are witnessing lingering clouds through hairy sewing arms of moose branches.

Nothing is uncommon as a hobby, but an incredible number of people aspire. To be still, to dream, to worry, to do nothing for a while. What a privilege, full of unpredictable data growth and so little wisdom, in this volatile and rapid age of knowledge. It's a gentle gift for yourself to do nothing.

What's in general a thorough walk, an old oak tree, or an afternoon of nothing? Each contributes to a uniquely personal experience that can anchor us and bring us back to a particular time and place—a highlight of our lives. Suppose it is physical abandonment when all of our energy comes to pass. In that case, absorption in nature lying on the ground to see a moving sky, or silence, not disturbed by one thing to do, not even speaking, we can give in to a peaceful inner place.

Might this be the ultimate "me" space?

My friend Julie will be traveling to Greece for a yoga workshop for her first Foreign journey. She has to decrypt schedules, signs, charts, and not all in her language by herself, as she travels alone. Julie knows that she will be called upon, and she is trustworthy of her inner guide, the "me." Julie has frequently spent time in meditation and reflection with this personal and peaceful space. Now she knows how to visit the space inside, to relax there, each time she visits, a feeling of personal renovation and restoration. And if a need occurs, it's puzzled or upset by the sign because a train has skipped, deceived by the wrong turn, it's able to go back to the quiet spot, to the safe place inside, over and over.

That's the spiritually awakening life. It is not an outwardly perfect existence, but it is exquisitely rich within once the individual claim your own holy "me" room.

Awakening The Divine Self

There is no deeper gift than one's self's dignity. ~Bars-Johnson Kate What does "honor yourself" mean? Some might consider it egoistic or egoist. Others may err for indulgence or "do whomever we want" because it feels good. Others might mistake it. In this writing, however, none of these views are valid. I want to convey today the understanding of honoring oneself by honoring the truth of who we are and taking from deep inside a level of Self-worth and self-acceptance. Overall else, it is our Self-worth that is our most precious, natural resource.

It is perfectly normal for us to feel dignified when I say 'natural.' That's how we come! But throughout our lives, we are always starting to question and doubt our worthiness, and our Self-admission starts to diminish. Simultaneously, the very part of our being, which we misuse, neglect, and kill, becomes our original valuable Self. In reality, there's nothing weaker than the pain that we afflict by negating who we are. However, we still do it: we move unwittingly away from our true existence, leave the Self, then want and expect someone else to come and recover us.

Many people spend their lives seeking ways to fill the gap left and become depressed and cynical because nothing and nothing can easily fill the void. Not because there is nobody to love them, but because nobody will love us as they are meant to love us. We have forgotten who we are really, and our job at hand is to remember when we avoid honoring, respecting, and validating ourselves. Nobody else will do it for us before we do. Many of us learn to live and deal with these subtle negative feelings and never associate them with a lack of self-reception or autonomy, but it still tells the guilty signs if we pay attention.

We might feel that something is missing. We can be self-conscious or paranoid, or we can judge others quickly. Before everyone has the chance, we beat ourselves with remorse and guilt and feel that we are responsible for the suffering of others. We also have several unsuccessful relationships or friendships or even employment. Often we are too arrogantly reassured, better at communicating with others, or excessively competitive and do not understand why our teams do not want people to participate. We may not express ourselves openly in our interpersonal relationships or question what we want, emotional and sexual, or in either case, we may be over-compensating for our fear.

These are all manifestations of a lack of self-worth and autonomy. As you can see, we harm our capacity, starting with our relationship with the Self, to establish safe and thriving world ties. This is not to suggest that we cannot recover and heal from these negative convictions about ourselves. If you realize this at this moment, know it: at the deepest stage of your consciousness, you know already that you are worthy, that you are loved, and that subtle longing that is just that true awakening in you, the glorious and beautiful truth, that you are, and have always been, worthy of love.

I urge you to start to look inside yourself, as you have purchased from others for too long, and look at how the doors of self-acceptability waver! If you honor your Self seems the least likely or reasonable thing to do, The heart of my life and work with others remains the root of that simple choice and, through it, I have learned that honoring my Self is honoring the Godhead. I'm so thankful for that! I hope you will also begin your journey to awaken, celebrate and honor your lovely Godself!

Spiritual Intelligence Real Secret

The Latin word spirit, meaning "breath," comes from the word spiritus. The breath of life is spirit. The Latin word intelligent means "choose between." Intelligentia is Latin. Our ability to choose between spirit and ego is spiritual intelligence. When we choose spirit over ego, compassion over fear, and the highest good for all egoistic interests, we actively practice spiritual wisdom.

The Voice of the Spirit is our Self's voice. My Self is the one who never left his maker. As One, every Higher Self is connected. Through my soul, I connect to my Superior Self. I dream of my soul — a part of my soul has gone through countless life experiences to get back to the Higher Self. My soul wants to wake up and recall who it is.

When I enter my soul and identify with my Higher Self, my Spirit, I grow my spiritual intelligence. I know that I'm not my body in this state of identity. I'm not my occupation or my gender. I'm not my people, and I'm not my religion. I am not the state of my life, disabilities, financial condition, or social status. I am not my problem, and I am not my history. Spiritual identity has me detaching from all ways and perceptions and seeing myself as a spiritual being in this human experience.

In spiritual circles, many people want to name the angels, Jesus, or other light creatures. That's fine. Many more use rituals, instruments, methodologies, and learning and development programs. It can also be healthy. We come to understand that we are the light when we grow spiritually. The light we're looking for you and me. We can't look for something that we have in us already. It cannot be done for us by an individual, program, or process. Nothing will get or awaken you from itself. Your purpose and determination lead you to the strength in you.

It's the true 'secret.' You don't need something out there. You already have in your love harmony, happiness, and wholeness. You have everything you need in the physical if you trust it completely. We form our source while hanging onto the form - the car, the home, the bank account, the big corps, and the great connection. God's Root is in us and is available forever. And that is the secret, and we're not apart from God.

We were born not knowing the secret in this universe. We don't have to be here if we knew it. However, we're here, so we need to learn something. Both the spirit-living trends and ego-live-living tendencies are manifest through the Law of Attraction in the physical world.

The movie and the novel, The Secret, inspire the law of attraction. You can certainly use the Law of Attraction to build the life you want. However, it should be noted that Hitler and Stalin used the law of attraction effectively. This film suggests that wealthy power brokers have always used the law of attraction. Spiritual intelligence enters into this field. You make it from spirit or ego when you create it?

The Secret makes another statement: "No one can do so." Another point. What do you do? Build a house of $4 million? Do you own more luxurious cars? A rich lifestyle living? If this is valid, we should infer that we who do not enjoy these wealthy are thinking somewhat wrong? On this basis, we should make Donald Trump, a principal instructor of our spirit, and Bill Gates the world guru.

In this life, each one of us has an independent intent. For others, they intend to have great wealth. It may not be for others. Some people are practicing change and swift results in their thoughts and emotions. Others have been doing so for 20 or 30 years and have not seen any improvements at all. There is no conclusion from either case where anyone knows it. The cause and the effect are not linearly linked. You probably won't think today about a negative thought, and something horrible will happen to you on the following day. You are the consciousness of your experience, knowledge, and intellect (or lack of it). The ego cannot foresee your life's physics.

You can have a deep problem with discouragement, for example. At the same time, you are safe, prosperous, and have successful relationships. You feel poor, notwithstanding your wealth and your health. In another case, the discouragement may be debt, ill health, hurtful ties, or all three. In reality, when you came to this life, you do not know what you signed up for. Cancer may appear because of deep rage, or you may have registered to learn something else about the cancer experience. We are not rewarding or punishing our life experiences. We have decided on a different level of awareness that there are development opportunities.

"Instead of being unhappy and poor, I shall be miserable and wealthy." I heard people say that. I heard people say. He's deceived. If you are really sad, wealth will give you a lot of fun, keeping you where you are. At the same time, you might be inspired to do the job with a lot of debt you have to deal with. You will be profoundly indebted and content with ecstatics. The debt is likely to disappear in time if you can retain your satisfaction. It is not the point, whether it is or not. What is significant is that there is inner richness, harmony, and joy within you, and you no longer identify with your manifestations. Nobody's more fortunate than you. The risk of seeking richness in your body before you have inner riches is that you believe that physical riches make you unique.

Great wealth, excellent health, and lovely relationships, but they are types. The form is affected. The form effects. It is the reason you concentrate on as a mind-smart being. At some stage in the process of spiritual growth, it seems necessary to have good stuff. You don't worry about anything anymore on your way.

Being an anti-materialist is no different from the wealthy person who identifies with his money by encouraging the picture that you are not only into things. The shape remains attentive. It doesn't make you special to be 'non-materialistic.' If you have many things or not is meaningless. What matters is that you can remove yourself from it and realize you have nothing. You're not your thing (or lack of stuff). You are a divine being on the way home to your Higher Self.

Your inner joy and prosperity are secretly secured by your divine understanding and your choice between spirit and ego—the three steps based on a book entitled the Song of Priests in Miracles. There is a wonderful 3 step method. In the first step, you give God a gift to all of your goals, problems, and concerns. You enter God in the song until you've drained yourself. That is, you recognize and dive into your Higher Self. In this situation, you know you are unconditionally blessed and cherished. The Echo is the third level. In other words, miracles will solve issues or help you reach your goals. Your capacity to let go and identify with the spirit is the true miracle. This produces inner richness, inner wellbeing, and inner love.

For our lives, we are 100% responsible. This means that we can respond by transferring our focus to our spiritual identity. No blame is placed on responsibilities. Power and opportunity are the responsibility. It's all: who's running your life at this very moment? Is it the ego or the spirit? Is love or is fear? Is it love? Your ego has its power if you feel anything other than calm. Remember that your body isn't your condition, not your body. You are an individual spiritual being. Your strength lies in that. In this thought, you know that little self-esteem, self-denial, and blame are illusions. You've told yourself these are just myths.

Be the real you. Be the real you. Where would you stand if you knew you were a strong spiritual being? How are you going to carry? What'd be your face's expression? What kind of thoughts would you allow? How would you behave if you knew you were loved unconditionally? What are you going to use for words? What would be your tone of voice? You exercise spiritual wisdom in this way. You are realizing, and so you are who you are.

This experience, awareness, and knowledge allow you to approach life with confidence. Trust is the basis of the effective application of the Law of Attraction. Your world reacts when you approach life with the highest confidence. Confidence based exclusively on externals or psychological information is fragile. Trust dependent on spiritual strength is strength.

This is the mystery that the universe has hidden from you—that you articulate God. Any moment you decide to live through your soul is an expensive and powerful moment. You affect others every time you make this choice. You are a light. You are a light. You're the world's blessing.

CONCLUSION

This is today's call for spiritual awakening.

It feels so amazing when I wake up spiritually. It feels like the presence of God. Since God is present all the time, I can only know its existence when I am tuned.

Do you feel like that too?

Do you want to shout at God sometimes and blame the Lord for all the wrong things in your life? How about accusing God of all the world's chaos! This is the best way to relieve God, Right! Right!

Do we sit down and pray to God and beg for a better life? Are we? Did we get it? Do we know who's got someone else? And our reply, what was it? The answer was, hopefully, good — one of consciousness and intelligence.

When we decide to wake up and become aware, our perspective is changed. Our divine beings in a physical world. How do I know? How do I know that? That's done here, been. I am clear that I am a spiritual being inside myself. A being of God-born light, so recognizing this reality feels amazing. This truth is strong. Wherever I ever am, I'm not just a happy hour. With my eyes opened or closed, I'm more than I can see.

How can I get my life better? How can our lives be improved?

Let us wake up to this very simple view of ourselves as spiritual beings. Our spirit is childlike, pitiful, powerful, lively, wise, happy, charismatic, expanding...

If we understand this reality about who we are really, all grace begins to open the doors to all goodness. Step by step, moment by moment, life will be recognized in a very meaningful way.

Why this commitment to this subject - GOD? For we remember ourselves when we recognize God. We will feel and identify ourselves as whole beings if we understand ourselves. Isn't it something that accomplishes us? Being entire? To be perfect!

We must be one with God to be thankful for what we are and have. Today and every day, let us all awaken to this truth to free our parent-born separation and allow God to bring us to him or her or live a very prosperous life in every way.

This life manifests spiritual revival to create good within and outside. We have conscious choices always, remember. Let all of us choose faiths that build integrity in themselves.

In Love, I express my humble gratitude, again and again, to this marvelous God and the whole universe for help in all circumstances. I love you. I love you. I love you. I love you. I love you. I love you.

You should share this insight so that the entire planet earth can spiritually awaken to create unity.

May love and light surround you, your loved ones, and the planet earth and God's whole universe, and guard, cure you.

When we unconditionally love, we will wake up to all of our eternal Blessings.